THIS JOURNAL BELONGS TO:

_____

THE LIT ON LIFE JOURNAL

A guide to
ignite a life
you love

THE LIT ON LIFE JOURNAL

Lexlee OVERTON

Copyright © 2021 by Lexlee Overton

All rights reserved. No part of this publication may be reproduced, distributed, stored in a retrieval system, or transmitted in any form or by any means, including photocopying, recording, or other electronic or mechanical methods, without the prior written permission of the author, except in the case of brief quotations embodied in critical reviews and certain other noncommercial uses permitted by copyright law.

ISBN: 978-1-7364177-0-6

Printed in the United States of America

Cover/interior design by Christy Collins, Constellation Book Services

THE LIT ON LIFE JOURNAL

Ignite Your Journey to Greatness, Now!

Welcome to the *Lit on Life Journal*, the journal for anyone who's ready to live life with more passion, energy and purpose.

By putting into practice what follows, you will step into dreaming bigger and achieving more, by taking consistent, focused action aligned with your personal mission and what matters to you.

As a mindset and energy coach, I've seen the results of harnessing our own energy to live more powerfully. I love sharing the most potent tools I've learned throughout my own journey to help others live intentionally, with the goal of being in love with life and creating change in the world.

The *Lit on Life Journal* is a proven system to help you be and achieve more. Using the exercises in this book, you will be able to begin each day with intention, end each day with reflection and shift throughout the day to stay aligned with your true mission.

Each day you will consistently move toward your goals, live your values and create exactly what you want.

Are you ready to ignite your life for greatness? Let's get started!

Be lit on life today and everyday,

Lexlee
OVERTON

Lexlee Overton—LitOnLife Founder and CEO

For additional resources, including free courses and videos, visit lexleeoverton.com

MOTIVATION IS WHAT GETS YOU STARTED.
COMMITMENT IS WHAT KEEPS YOU GOING.

Write a letter to yourself describing your commitment over the next 13 weeks. Be very specific about what you want to create, how you will be accountable and how your life will change.

Dear _____, (your name)

I promise to...

I will create...

I will hold myself accountable by...

I know my life will change by...

Signature   Date

FOUNDATIONS

We begin our 13 week journey with an overview of the five pillars that you will learn about and use as your energetic foundation to build the life you love. The second part of the journal consists of 13 weeks worth of worksheets and exercises to keep you accountable and motivated on your journey.

1. MAP OUT CORE VALUE GOALS

First, you will create goals that align with your deepest values. These goals will serve as the guide by which you'll know how to best spend your time and invest your energy, as well as which relationships really matter and deserve your attention. Your life will no longer be about merely reacting to what comes your way. Rather, you will face each day with the energy to create in a way that aligns with what is most important to you.

2. CRAFT A COMPELLING PERSONAL MISSION

Next, you'll get clear on what matters most to you and then design a blueprint that will guide you towards success in those (and other) areas of your life. Drafting a personal mission statement helps you to hone in on what you stand for and what you believe in, which will then aid you to create goals that propel you toward your vision. Once you are clear on your mission, you'll stop wondering what you should be doing and stop wishing you were doing life differently.

3. USE YOUR ENERGY WITH INTENTION

You have a limited amount of energy to invest in your life. It's time to start planning how to best utilize that energy. You will also learn daily practices geared towards fueling your energy so you can create more purpose, joy and fulfillment.

4. EMBRACE AWARENESS AND REFLECTION

Creating change takes awareness. You must choose to become consciously aware of who you are and where you are going if you want to do life differently. To keep yourself focused, you'll find space for weekly and daily tracking of your thoughts, actions and habits. You will also reflect on special questions meant to boost your mood and propel you forward as you live out your vision.

5. CONSISTENT POSITIVE ENERGY

You'll greet the morning with intention, choosing who you are and what you want from each day. You will use daily gratitude to reinforce your energy and shift your mind and emotions for more power. You will eliminate the negativity of anxiety before it starts. You will adopt an energetic setpoint where nothing is impossible.

Now that you have an overview, let's dive into igniting your 13 week journey for greatness!

Your
core values
are the beliefs
that describe
your soul.

#LitOnLife

MAP OUT CORE VALUES

Values are the principles or standards that represent what is important in your life.

Your values should...

- drive your behavior
- reflect the energy of your deepest dreams
- include what matters most to you in how you live your life
- become a personal guide for everything you do

By gaining clarity about your values, you'll gain clarity about yourself, be able to easily define your priorities and obtain insight into what you really want out of your life.

Let's start right now with some personal reflection. Grab a pen and write down any key words that come to mind as you explore the following prompts.

First, think about who you really want to be and what you stand for. What's most important in your life? Beyond your basic human needs, what must you have in your life in order to experience fulfillment? For example, do you need...

> - a source of creative self-expression
> - a strong level of health and vitality
> - a sense of excitement and adventure
> - to be surrounded by beauty
> - to always be learning
> - to love unconditionally
> - to be of service

What do you stand for?

Which personal values must you honor, or else a part of you withers?

What values are essential to your life?

What values represent your primary way of being?

What values are essential to supporting your inner self?

Think of someone you admire. What qualities or values do they live or exhibit?

CRAFT VALUE STATEMENTS

Now you will use the output of your brainstorming to create the value statements which will serve as your core set of guiding principles.

Highlighting and then merging the key thoughts generated above into memorable phrases or sentences can help you to articulate the meaning behind each value. It also gives you the opportunity to make the value more emotional and memorable.

Here are a few tips and guidelines for crafting your values statements:

- Use inspiring words and vocabulary. Our brains are quick to delete or ignore the mundane and commonplace.
- Search for words that evoke and trigger emotional responses.
- Make your value statements rich and meaningful to you so they inspire you to uphold them.

You can have more than one value statement to define your core values.

EXAMPLES OF CORE VALUES AND STRONG VALUE STATEMENTS

Core Value: Teaching
Value Statement: I believe in creating change by learning, growing and sharing wisdom.

Core Value: Connection
Value Statement: Lives are changed when we remember that how we think, speak and act affects everyone. My energy affects all.

Now, you try...

Value #1:_____ **Value #2:**_____
Value Statement #1 **Value Statement #2:**

Value #3:_____ **Value #4:**_____
Value Statement #3 **Value Statement #4:**

Value #5:_____
Value Statement #5

After writing your value statements, ask yourself:

Does this define me?

Is this who I am at my best? Is this a filter that I can use to make hard decisions?

Be
The Energy
You Want
to Attract

#LitOnLife

CRAFT A COMPELLING PERSONAL MISSION

PART 1

1. When you were 5 years old, what did you want to be when you grew up? Why? How did you think it would make your future self feel?

2. When you were 15 years old, what did you want to be when you grew up? Why? How did you think it would make your future self feel?

3. What excites you in or about the world?

4. What angers you in or about the world?

5. Think about your answer to question 3. If you could share three things that excite you with others, what would you want to share or teach?

6. Think about your answer to question 4. If you could convey three things that anger you, what would you convey?

7. Make a list of experiences or subjects you are curious to learn more about.

PART 2

1. What makes you smile? (Activities, people, events, hobbies, projects, etc.)

2. What were your favorite things to do in the past? What about now?

3. What activities make you lose track of time?

4. What makes you feel great about yourself?

5. Who inspires you most? (It could be anyone you know or do not know, such as family, friends, authors, artists, leaders, etc.) Which qualities inspire you about each person?

6. What are you naturally good at? (Skills, abilities, gifts etc.)

7. What do people typically ask you for help with?

PART 3

It's time to put it all together, and use your values, your past successes and the things that excite and anger you to write your personal mission statement.

Example:

Lexlee's Mission Statement: The purpose of my life is to teach, serve and heal through love while building communities of support and inspiration.

Draft Your Personal Mission Statement:

YOUR MISSION GOALS

Now it's time to create goals based on your newly crafted mission statement. These are not specific, task-oriented goals, rather they are part of your mission and will help you determine how and where to invest your energy. Mission goals will help you answer "yes" or "no" when faced with anything from simple daily actions to big life decisions.

Review your mission statement and break it down into three core mission goals.

Example:
Lexlee's Mission Statement: The purpose of my life is to teach, serve and heal through love while building communities of support and inspiration.

Mission Goal #1: Teaching

Mission Goal #2: Service

Mission Goal #3: Connection

After identifying your mission goals, take a moment to reflect and define what each means to you and how each may appear in different areas of your life.

Example:

Lexlee's Mission Goal #1: Teaching
Definition: It is important to my mission to continuously learn and then, in turn, teach others how to be more empowered in their authentic truths. My mission is supported by the goal of learning new ways to shift energy, grow personally and teach my children, family and others how to do the same.

Mission Goal #2: Service
Definition: My life's mission is fulfilled when my work is heart-centered and about helping others.

Mission Goal #3: Connection
Definition: My mission is deepened by creating communities that support and inspire each other to grow and heal.

Write Your Mission Goals:

Mission Goal #1

Mission Goal #2

Mission Goal #3

Dare to
Live Your LIfe
With
Boldness

#LitOnLIfe

USING ENERGY WITH INTENTION: VISUALIZATION

Visualization is one of the most powerful techniques to shift energy toward your vision. Although visualization is about creating mental pictures of an outcome, the trick to this practice is to explore the *feelings* around attaining your goal.

Let's say your goal is to get a pay raise. You can probably envision yourself requesting the raise and then see yourself celebrating when you get it. But to make this exercise even more energetically powerful, you must identify the emotions associated with the goal. Maybe those emotions are feelings of abundance, being valued or feeling excited? Whatever they may be, allow yourself to truly *feel* the success of your goal.

Create visualizations for each of your mission goals. First, identify how the success of achievement might *feel* in the moment. Then, journal about what success could look like. Be detailed and bring in all five senses. What do you see? What's going on? Are you being congratulated? Is someone cheering you on? How are you celebrating?

Remember, this is just a written practice to jump-start your imagination, so don't put too much pressure on yourself. When you practice daily visualization, your mind may create even more detailed and different scenes.

Mission Goal # 1 Visualization:

Feelings:_____

Detailed Picture:

Mission Goal # 2 Visualization:

Feelings:_____

Detailed Picture:

Mission Goal #3 Visualization:

Feelings:_____

Write a Detailed Picture:

The way we
spend our time
defines
who we are.

#LitOnLIfe

USING ENERGY WITH INTENTION: WEEKLY VISION

Step into the powerful practice of intentionally planning how, where, and with whom you invest your energy each week.

An impactful weekly vision is shaped by a three part process. First, you create awareness of your desires, obligations and commitments. Then, you focus your energy on those actions that align with your mission and goals. Lastly, you plan for the unexpected.

PART 1: THE MUST DO LIST

You will begin each week by getting real about what *must* be done. This practice brings into clear focus what really needs to happen in our lives.

On this list, you will include only the actions that MUST happen in the coming week.

1. Start by listing this week's must dos. This list is only for the appointments, commitments or deadlines *already scheduled* for the week.
2. Next, write down the date and time of the must do item.
3. Estimate how long it will take to complete each task.
4. Once you finish your must do list, input the necessary actions into your calendar to keep you committed and focused with your time.

EXAMPLE MUST DO LIST:

Must Do This Week	Scheduled Time or Due Date	Estimate Time to Complete
Meeting with client	Thursday at 9:00 a.m.	1 hour
Complete Motion for Summary Judgment	Friday by close of business	3 hours
Take my son to dentist	Tuesday at 4:00 p.m.	1 hour

PART 2: THE BRAIN DUMP

1. **Brain Dump.** Write down everything currently on your mind that is *not* due this week. This list includes all of those non-must dos that should be done or that would be nice to get to. Allow your mind to dump it all on the page.

    ➤ **Examples:** Create a persuasive and effective marketing campaign, prepare for next month's trial, organize home space, take car in for an oil change.

2. **Mission Goal or Devil's Vortex?** Go through the list. For each item, ask yourself if the action aligns with and/or furthers your mission goals? Does the task fit under one of the mission goals you created earlier? If so, note which mission goal the action furthers. If not, recognize that this activity might fall under the Devil's Vortex. This is a category of actions that we perform but that don't necessarily further our mission goals. Such activities should be delegated or eliminated rather than using your energy to complete.

3. **Automate/Delegate/Eliminate/Schedule.** For each item, decide which of the following applies:

    ➤ **Automate.** This type of item should happen like clockwork, so you need to create a system for automation. Let's say you need to meet with your team every week. To automate this task, set a time for the meeting each week and lock it in the calendar. For example, team meetings will happen every Monday at 9:00 a.m.

- **Delegate.** Ask yourself, "Can someone else do this task instead of me?" If the answer is yes, delegate it to someone else, if possible. For example, if you don't have time to pick up dry cleaning, delegate it to someone else, such as your spouse or an assistant.
- **Eliminate.** This is an item that you don't need to do in the near future, or possibly ever. For example, if you "need to" clean out the garage, you might realize that it's not necessary this year and can eliminate it from your list.
- **Schedule.** If an item on your brain dump list cannot be automated, eliminated or delegated then you need to schedule time to complete it.
- Prioritize the importance of each item to be scheduled, using one of the following designations.

    - Must be done this week
    - Must be done next week
    - Must be done this month
    - Next month
    - Next 3 months

Next, block the tasks accordingly on your calendar.

Item	Mission Goal or Devil's Vortex?	Due Date/Desired Completion Date	Estimated Time to Complete	Automate/Delegate Eliminate/Schedule
Start meeting with my team weekly	Mission 3: Connection	N/A	1 Hour	A
Pick up dry cleaning	Devil's Vortex	This week	30 minutes	D
Clean out garage	Devil's Vortex	None	5 hours	E
Prepare next month's trial	Mission 2: Service	Trial Date	30 hours	S

PART 3: PLAN FOR THE UNEXPECTED

As we all know, the best laid plans can often go awry. The best way to plan for the unexpected is to, well, expect it.

> **Schedule the Unexpected.** Each day, block time for the unexpected, such as unscheduled client calls, urgent emails, or new client meetings. Try to block one hour in the morning or afternoon to cover these kinds of interruptions.

> **Build in Breaks.** Build time into your daily schedule to recharge. For optimal performance throughout the day, you need to take time to reset, reflect and recharge. Schedule a quick recharging break after every hour of focused work. Try quick breathing practices or a grounding meditation. For resources on how to quickly recharge your energy, visit www.litonlife.com.

Our words have manifesting power. You can change your world by changing your words.

#LitOnLife

USING ENERGY WITH INTENTION: POWER WORDS AND QUESTIONS

Our energy is a combination of our physical, mental and emotional states. Everything is energy. Your thoughts are energy and can either be used as a weapon against you or as a powerful tool to fuel your power.

Every day, you will be guided to choose a power word. This word will serve as an intention for your energy. How will you choose to think, feel and see the world? Will you be empowered, excited, happy, and focused? Or, will you be anxious, fearful, worried, or unintentional? You will use your power word to define who you are each day.

On a designated day each week, you will also reflect upon power questions. Answering these questions can help to shift your mood and, thus, your energy. These questions are meant to steer you toward the direction of your desires. Your power questions will give you the energy you need to face challenges and stay on track.

CONSISTENT POSITIVE ENERGY: THE DAILY CORE FOUR

These high-vibe activities are designed to fuel your physical, mental and emotional energy! Each day, aim to spend 15 minutes on *each* of the following activities.

Core Activity #1

MOVE: Move your body in some way for 15 minutes each day. Physical movement is a great way to shift and jump-start your energy. There is no limit to the range of activities, the only essential requirement is that you move! Some suggested moves include breathing practices, yoga or other stretching exercises, walking, running, weight lifting, bike riding, or hiking.

Core Activity #2

CLEAR: Spend 15 minutes clearing or organizing some space in your physical environment. Our surroundings absorb our energy, physically and emotionally. To keep the vibe high, it is important to declutter and clean to keep our space energetically clear. For this core activity, choose any clearing, organizing or cleaning project that helps you to feel more grounded. Options include organizing a closet, cleaning the kitchen, or clearing off your desk.

Core Activity #3

CONNECT: Scientific studies show that one of the key factors to happiness is to develop meaningful relationships. The quantity of relationships is not what matters, rather the meaning of and connection within the relationships. For this core activity, focus on connecting with one person for at least 15 minutes. Connection may mean being present without your phone or actively listening or it may mean talking to someone you haven't seen for a long time. You choose, all that matters is the choice is to connect.

Core Activity #4

LOVE: This core activity is simple. Do something you love for 15 minutes. Maybe it's reading, taking a hot bath, walking the dog or cooking something delicious! Just have fun!

Monthly Overview

JANUARY
S	M	T	W	T	F	S
					1	2
3	4	5	6	7	8	9
10	11	12	13	14	15	16
17	18	19	20	21	22	23
24	25	26	27	28	29	30
31						

FEBRUARY
S	M	T	W	T	F	S
	1	2	3	4	5	6
7	8	9	10	11	12	13
14	15	16	17	18	19	20
21	22	23	24	25	26	27
28						

MARCH
S	M	T	W	T	F	S
	1	2	3	4	5	6
7	8	9	10	11	12	13
14	15	16	17	18	19	20
21	22	23	24	25	26	27
28	29	30	31			

APRIL
S	M	T	W	T	F	S
				1	2	3
4	5	6	7	8	9	10
11	12	13	14	15	16	17
18	19	20	21	22	23	24
25	26	27	28	29	30	

MAY
S	M	T	W	T	F	S
						1
2	3	4	5	6	7	8
9	10	11	12	13	14	15
16	17	18	19	20	21	22
23	24	25	26	27	28	29
30	31					

JUNE
S	M	T	W	T	F	S
		1	2	3	4	5
6	7	8	9	10	11	12
13	14	15	16	17	18	19
20	21	22	23	24	25	26
27	28	29	30			

JULY
S	M	T	W	T	F	S
				1	2	3
4	5	6	7	8	9	10
11	12	13	14	15	16	17
18	19	20	21	22	23	24
25	26	27	28	29	30	31

AUGUST
S	M	T	W	T	F	S
1	2	3	4	5	6	7
8	9	10	11	12	13	14
15	16	17	18	19	20	21
22	23	24	25	26	27	28
29	30	31				

SEPTEMBER
S	M	T	W	T	F	S
			1	2	3	4
5	6	7	8	9	10	11
12	13	14	15	16	17	18
19	20	21	22	23	24	25
26	27	28	29	30		

OCTOBER

S	M	T	W	T	F	S
					1	2
3	4	5	6	7	8	9
10	11	12	13	14	15	16
17	18	19	20	21	22	23
24	25	26	27	28	29	30
31						

NOVEMBER
S	M	T	W	T	F	S
	1	2	3	4	5	6
7	8	9	10	11	12	13
14	15	16	17	18	19	20
21	22	23	24	25	26	27
28	29	30				

DECEMBER
S	M	T	W	T	F	S
			1	2	3	4
5	6	7	8	9	10	11
12	13	14	15	16	17	18
19	20	21	22	23	24	25
26	27	28	29	30	31	

Month of _____

SUN	MON	TUES	WED	THU	FRI	SAT

Priorities for the Month of

NOTES

WEEK ONE

The power to create begins with clear vision.

#LitOnLife

Weekly Vision

WEEK

Week of: _____ / _____

Weekly Power Word:

How can I step into this intention this week?

Must Do List: Events and Deadlines

Must Do This Week	Schedule Time or Due Date	Estimate Time to Complete

Brain Dump:

Write down everything currently on your mind that is not due this week.

Item	Mission Goal or Devil's Vortex?	Due Date/Desired Completion Date	Estimated Time to Complete	Automate/Delegate Eliminate/Schedule

Connections You Would Like to Grow This Week:

....

....

....

Weekly Visualizations

Goal   How would it feel?

1: ....

2: ....

3: ....

Weekly Review

Week of: _____ / _____

Weekly Reflections:

Wins, Celebrations, Highlights

_____
_____
_____

Lowlights, Lessons Learned

_____
_____
_____

What thoughts, actions and habits worked well this week?

_____
_____
_____

What thoughts, actions and habits do you want to change?

_____
_____
_____

Weekly Power Question

What are 3 energy drains you want to focus on stopping now?

_____
_____
_____
_____

Ⓢ Ⓜ Ⓣ Ⓦ Ⓣ Ⓕ Ⓢ   Date _____/_____

Morning Energy Questions

Energy

Daily Power Word:

_____

Physical Goal

Today, I will care and nurture
my body by:

_____

_____

_____

Mindset

Today, I'm grateful for:

_____

_____

_____

Heartset

What can I do for others today?

_____

_____

_____

Daily Core Four

15 minutes each

○ Move
○ Clear
○ Connect
○ Love

5:00 _____
6:00 _____
7:00 _____
8:00 _____
9:00 _____
10:00 _____
11:00 _____
12:00 _____
1:00 _____
2:00 _____
3:00 _____
4:00 _____
5:00 _____
6:00 _____
7:00 _____
8:00 _____
9:00 _____
10:00 _____
11:00 _____

Visualization of Mission Goals

Mission Goal #1: _____

Mission Goal #2: _____

Mission Goal #3: _____

Evening Energy Questions

What went great today? (Wins and Celebrations)
_____
_____
_____
_____
_____

What would I do differently tomorrow?
_____
_____
_____
_____
_____

Ⓢ Ⓜ Ⓣ Ⓦ Ⓣ Ⓕ Ⓢ   Date _____ / _____

Morning Energy Questions

Energy

Daily Power Word:

_____

Physical Goal

Today, I will care and nurture
my body by:

_____

_____

_____

Mindset

Today, I'm grateful for:

_____

_____

_____

Heartset

What can I do for others today?

_____

_____

_____

Daily Core Four

15 minutes each

○ Move
○ Clear
○ Connect
○ Love

5:00 _____
6:00 _____
7:00 _____
8:00 _____
9:00 _____
10:00 _____
11:00 _____
12:00 _____
1:00 _____
2:00 _____
3:00 _____
4:00 _____
5:00 _____
6:00 _____
7:00 _____
8:00 _____
9:00 _____
10:00 _____
11:00 _____

Visualization of Mission Goals

Mission Goal #1: ....

Mission Goal #2: ....

Mission Goal #3: ....

Evening Energy Questions

What went great today? (Wins and Celebrations)

....

....

....

....

What would I do differently tomorrow?

....

....

....

....

Ⓢ Ⓜ Ⓣ Ⓦ Ⓣ Ⓕ Ⓢ   Date _____ / _____

Morning Energy Questions

Energy

Daily Power Word:

_____

Physical Goal

Today, I will care and nurture
my body by:

_____

_____

_____

Mindset

Today, I'm grateful for:

_____

_____

_____

Heartset

What can I do for others today?

_____

_____

_____

Daily Core Four

15 minutes each

○ Move
○ Clear
○ Connect
○ Love

5:00 _____
6:00 _____
7:00 _____
8:00 _____
9:00 _____
10:00 _____
11:00 _____
12:00 _____
1:00 _____
2:00 _____
3:00 _____
4:00 _____
5:00 _____
6:00 _____
7:00 _____
8:00 _____
9:00 _____
10:00 _____
11:00 _____

Visualization of Mission Goals

Mission Goal #1: _____

Mission Goal #2: _____

Mission Goal #3: _____

Evening Energy Questions

What went great today? (Wins and Celebrations)

_____
_____
_____
_____
_____

What would I do differently tomorrow?

_____
_____
_____
_____
_____

Ⓢ Ⓜ Ⓣ Ⓦ Ⓣ Ⓕ Ⓢ   Date _____ / _____

Morning Energy Questions

Energy

Daily Power Word:

_____

Physical Goal

Today, I will care and nurture
my body by:

_____

_____

_____

Mindset

Today, I'm grateful for:

_____

_____

_____

Heartset

What can I do for others today?

_____

_____

Daily Core Four

15 minutes each

- ○ Move
- ○ Clear
- ○ Connect
- ○ Love

5:00 _____
6:00 _____
7:00 _____
8:00 _____
9:00 _____
10:00 _____
11:00 _____
12:00 _____
1:00 _____
2:00 _____
3:00 _____
4:00 _____
5:00 _____
6:00 _____
7:00 _____
8:00 _____
9:00 _____
10:00 _____
11:00 _____

Visualization of Mission Goals

Mission Goal #1: _____

Mission Goal #2: _____

Mission Goal #3: _____

Evening Energy Questions

What went great today? (Wins and Celebrations)

_____
_____
_____
_____

What would I do differently tomorrow?

_____
_____
_____
_____

Ⓢ Ⓜ Ⓣ Ⓦ Ⓣ Ⓕ Ⓢ   Date _____/_____

Morning Energy Questions

Energy

Daily Power Word:

....

Physical Goal

Today, I will care and nurture
my body by:

....

....

....

Mindset

Today, I'm grateful for:

....

....

....

Heartset

What can I do for others today?

....

....

5:00 ....
6:00 ....
7:00 ....
8:00 ....
9:00 ....
10:00 ....
11:00 ....
12:00 ....
1:00 ....
2:00 ....
3:00 ....
4:00 ....
5:00 ....
6:00 ....
7:00 ....
8:00 ....
9:00 ....
10:00 ....
11:00 ....

Daily Core Four

15 minutes each
○ Move
○ Clear
○ Connect
○ Love

Visualization of Mission Goals

Mission Goal #1: ....

Mission Goal #2: ....

Mission Goal #3: ....

Evening Energy Questions

What went great today? (Wins and Celebrations)
....
....
....
....
....

What would I do differently tomorrow?
....
....
....
....

Ⓢ Ⓜ Ⓣ Ⓦ Ⓣ Ⓕ Ⓢ   Date _____ / _____

Morning Energy Questions

Energy

Daily Power Word:

....

Physical Goal

Today, I will care and nurture my body by:

....

....

....

Mindset

Today, I'm grateful for:

....

....

....

Heartset

What can I do for others today?

....

....

....

Daily Core Four

15 minutes each

○ Move
○ Clear
○ Connect
○ Love

5:00 _____
6:00 _____
7:00 _____
8:00 _____
9:00 _____
10:00 _____
11:00 _____
12:00 _____
1:00 _____
2:00 _____
3:00 _____
4:00 _____
5:00 _____
6:00 _____
7:00 _____
8:00 _____
9:00 _____
10:00 _____
11:00 _____

Visualization of Mission Goals

Mission Goal #1: ....

Mission Goal #2: ....

Mission Goal #3: ....

Evening Energy Questions

What went great today? (Wins and Celebrations)

....

....

....

....

What would I do differently tomorrow?

....

....

....

....

Ⓢ Ⓜ Ⓣ Ⓦ Ⓣ Ⓕ Ⓢ   Date _____ / _____

Morning Energy Questions

Energy

Daily Power Word:

Physical Goal

Today, I will care and nurture
my body by:

Mindset

Today, I'm grateful for:

Heartset

What can I do for others today?

Daily Core Four

15 minutes each

- ○ Move
- ○ Clear
- ○ Connect
- ○ Love

5:00 _____
6:00 _____
7:00 _____
8:00 _____
9:00 _____
10:00 _____
11:00 _____
12:00 _____
1:00 _____
2:00 _____
3:00 _____
4:00 _____
5:00 _____
6:00 _____
7:00 _____
8:00 _____
9:00 _____
10:00 _____
11:00 _____

Visualization of Mission Goals

Mission Goal #1: ....

Mission Goal #2: ....

Mission Goal #3: ....

Evening Energy Questions

What went great today? (Wins and Celebrations)

....

....

....

....

What would I do differently tomorrow?

....

....

....

....

WEEK TWO

It's time to ignite a fire within you to finally step into all you dream of becoming.

#LitOnLife

Weekly Vision

WEEK

Week of: _____ / _____

Weekly Power Word:

How can I step into this intention this week?

Must Do List: Events and Deadlines

Must Do This Week	Schedule Time or Due Date	Estimate Time to Complete

Brain Dump:

Write down everything currently on your mind that is not due this week.

Item	Mission Goal or Devil's Vortex?	Due Date/Desired Completion Date	Estimated Time to Complete	Automate/Delegate Eliminate/Schedule

Connections You Would Like to Grow This Week:

....

....

....

Weekly Visualizations

Goal   How would it feel?

1: ....

2: ....

3: ....

Weekly Review

WEEK

Week of: _____ / _____

Weekly Reflections:

Wins, Celebrations, Highlights

....
....
....

Lowlights, Lessons Learned

....
....
....

What thoughts, actions and habits worked well this week?

....
....
....

What thoughts, actions and habits do you want to change?

....
....
....

Weekly Power Question

Describe 5 qualities you love about yourself.

....
....
....
....

Ⓢ Ⓜ Ⓣ Ⓦ Ⓣ Ⓕ Ⓢ

Date _____ /_____

Morning Energy Questions

Energy

Daily Power Word:

_____

Physical Goal

Today, I will care and nurture
my body by:

_____

_____

_____

Mindset

Today, I'm grateful for:

_____

_____

_____

Heartset

What can I do for others today?

_____

_____

_____

Daily Core Four

15 minutes each

○ Move
○ Clear
○ Connect
○ Love

5:00 _____
6:00 _____
7:00 _____
8:00 _____
9:00 _____
10:00 _____
11:00 _____
12:00 _____
1:00 _____
2:00 _____
3:00 _____
4:00 _____
5:00 _____
6:00 _____
7:00 _____
8:00 _____
9:00 _____
10:00 _____
11:00 _____

Visualization of Mission Goals

Mission Goal #1: _____

Mission Goal #2: _____

Mission Goal #3: _____

Evening Energy Questions

What went great today? (Wins and Celebrations)
_____
_____
_____
_____

What would I do differently tomorrow?
_____
_____
_____
_____

Ⓢ Ⓜ Ⓣ Ⓦ Ⓣ Ⓕ Ⓢ   Date _____ / _____

Morning Energy Questions

Energy

Daily Power Word:

....

Physical Goal

Today, I will care and nurture
my body by:

....

....

....

Mindset

Today, I'm grateful for:

....

....

....

Heartset

What can I do for others today?

....

....

....

Daily Core Four

15 minutes each

○ Move

○ Clear

○ Connect

○ Love

5:00 ....
6:00 ....
7:00 ....
8:00 ....
9:00 ....
10:00 ....
11:00 ....
12:00 ....
1:00 ....
2:00 ....
3:00 ....
4:00 ....
5:00 ....
6:00 ....
7:00 ....
8:00 ....
9:00 ....
10:00 ....
11:00 ....

Visualization of Mission Goals

Mission Goal #1: ....

Mission Goal #2: ....

Mission Goal #3: ....

Evening Energy Questions

What went great today? (Wins and Celebrations)

....

....

....

....

What would I do differently tomorrow?

....

....

....

....

Ⓢ Ⓜ Ⓣ Ⓦ Ⓣ Ⓕ Ⓢ   Date _____/_____

Morning Energy Questions

Energy

Daily Power Word:

_____

Physical Goal

Today, I will care and nurture my body by:

_____

_____

_____

Mindset

Today, I'm grateful for:

_____

_____

_____

Heartset

What can I do for others today?

_____

_____

_____

Daily Core Four

15 minutes each

○ Move
○ Clear
○ Connect
○ Love

5:00 _____
6:00 _____
7:00 _____
8:00 _____
9:00 _____
10:00 _____
11:00 _____
12:00 _____
1:00 _____
2:00 _____
3:00 _____
4:00 _____
5:00 _____
6:00 _____
7:00 _____
8:00 _____
9:00 _____
10:00 _____
11:00 _____

Visualization of Mission Goals

Mission Goal #1:

Mission Goal #2:

Mission Goal #3:

Evening Energy Questions

What went great today? (Wins and Celebrations)

What would I do differently tomorrow?

Ⓢ Ⓜ Ⓣ Ⓦ Ⓣ Ⓕ Ⓢ   Date _____ / _____

Morning Energy Questions

Energy

Daily Power Word:

_____

Physical Goal

Today, I will care and nurture
my body by:

_____

_____

_____

Mindset

Today, I'm grateful for:

_____

_____

_____

Heartset

What can I do for others today?

_____

_____

_____

Daily Core Four
15 minutes each

○ Move

○ Clear

○ Connect

○ Love

5:00 _____

6:00 _____

7:00 _____

8:00 _____

9:00 _____

10:00 _____

11:00 _____

12:00 _____

1:00 _____

2:00 _____

3:00 _____

4:00 _____

5:00 _____

6:00 _____

7:00 _____

8:00 _____

9:00 _____

10:00 _____

11:00 _____

Visualization of Mission Goals

Mission Goal #1: ....

Mission Goal #2: ....

Mission Goal #3: ....

Evening Energy Questions

What went great today? (Wins and Celebrations)

....

....

....

....

What would I do differently tomorrow?

....

....

....

....

S M T W T F S   Date _____ / _____

Morning Energy Questions

Energy

Daily Power Word:

....

Physical Goal

Today, I will care and nurture
my body by:

....

....

....

Mindset

Today, I'm grateful for:

....

....

....

Heartset

What can I do for others today?

....

....

....

Daily Core Four

15 minutes each

○ Move

○ Clear

○ Connect

○ Love

5:00 ....
6:00 ....
7:00 ....
8:00 ....
9:00 ....
10:00 ....
11:00 ....
12:00 ....
1:00 ....
2:00 ....
3:00 ....
4:00 ....
5:00 ....
6:00 ....
7:00 ....
8:00 ....
9:00 ....
10:00 ....
11:00 ....

Visualization of Mission Goals

Mission Goal #1: _____

Mission Goal #2: _____

Mission Goal #3: _____

Evening Energy Questions

What went great today? (Wins and Celebrations)

_____
_____
_____
_____

What would I do differently tomorrow?

_____
_____
_____
_____

(S) (M) (T) (W) (T) (F) (S)   Date _____ / _____

Morning Energy Questions

Energy

Daily Power Word:

_____

Physical Goal

Today, I will care and nurture
my body by:

_____

_____

Mindset

Today, I'm grateful for:

_____

_____

Heartset

What can I do for others today?

_____

_____

Daily Core Four

15 minutes each

○ Move
○ Clear
○ Connect
○ Love

5:00 _____
6:00 _____
7:00 _____
8:00 _____
9:00 _____
10:00 _____
11:00 _____
12:00 _____
1:00 _____
2:00 _____
3:00 _____
4:00 _____
5:00 _____
6:00 _____
7:00 _____
8:00 _____
9:00 _____
10:00 _____
11:00 _____

Visualization of Mission Goals

Mission Goal #1: ....

Mission Goal #2: ....

Mission Goal #3: ....

Evening Energy Questions

What went great today? (Wins and Celebrations)

....
....
....
....

What would I do differently tomorrow?

....
....
....
....

S M T W T F S   Date _____ / _____

Morning Energy Questions

Energy
Daily Power Word:
....

Physical Goal
Today, I will care and nurture
my body by:
....
....
....

Mindset
Today, I'm grateful for:
....
....
....

Heartset
What can I do for others today?
....
....
....

Daily Core Four
15 minutes each
- ○ Move
- ○ Clear
- ○ Connect
- ○ Love

5:00 ....
6:00 ....
7:00 ....
8:00 ....
9:00 ....
10:00 ....
11:00 ....
12:00 ....
1:00 ....
2:00 ....
3:00 ....
4:00 ....
5:00 ....
6:00 ....
7:00 ....
8:00 ....
9:00 ....
10:00 ....
11:00 ....

Visualization of Mission Goals

Mission Goal #1: ....

Mission Goal #2: ....

Mission Goal #3: ....

Evening Energy Questions

What went great today? (Wins and Celebrations)

....

....

....

....

What would I do differently tomorrow?

....

....

....

....

WEEK THREE

I believe in infinite possible destinies.

#LitOnLife

Weekly Vision

WEEK 3

Week of: _____ / _____

Weekly Power Word:

....

How can I step into this intention this week?

....

....

Must Do List: Events and Deadlines

Must Do This Week	Schedule Time or Due Date	Estimate Time to Complete

Brain Dump:

Write down everything currently on your mind that is not due this week.

Item	Mission Goal or Devil's Vortex?	Due Date/Desired Completion Date	Estimated Time to Complete	Automate/Delegate Eliminate/Schedule

Connections You Would Like to Grow This Week:

....

....

....

Weekly Visualizations

Goal   How would it feel?

1: ....

2: ....

3: ....

Weekly Review

WEEK

Week of: _____ / _____

Weekly Reflections:

Wins, Celebrations, Highlights

....

....

....

Lowlights, Lessons Learned

....

....

....

What thoughts, actions and habits worked well this week?

....

....

....

What thoughts, actions and habits do you want to change?

....

....

....

Weekly Power Question

When you are in pain, physical or emotional, the kindest thing you can do for yourself is...?

....

....

....

....

(S) (M) (T) (W) (T) (F) (S)	Date _____ / _____

Morning Energy Questions

Energy
Daily Power Word:

_____

Physical Goal
Today, I will care and nurture
my body by:

_____

_____

_____

Mindset
Today, I'm grateful for:

_____

_____

_____

Heartset
What can I do for others today?

_____

_____

_____

Daily Core Four
15 minutes each
- ○ Move
- ○ Clear
- ○ Connect
- ○ Love

5:00 _____
6:00 _____
7:00 _____
8:00 _____
9:00 _____
10:00 _____
11:00 _____
12:00 _____
1:00 _____
2:00 _____
3:00 _____
4:00 _____
5:00 _____
6:00 _____
7:00 _____
8:00 _____
9:00 _____
10:00 _____
11:00 _____

Visualization of Mission Goals

Mission Goal #1: ....

Mission Goal #2: ....

Mission Goal #3: ....

Evening Energy Questions

What went great today? (Wins and Celebrations)
....
....
....
....

What would I do differently tomorrow?
....
....
....
....

Ⓢ Ⓜ Ⓣ Ⓦ Ⓣ Ⓕ Ⓢ   Date _____ / _____

Morning Energy Questions

Energy

Daily Power Word:

....

Physical Goal

Today, I will care and nurture
my body by:

....

....

....

Mindset

Today, I'm grateful for:

....

....

....

Heartset

What can I do for others today?

....

....

....

Daily Core Four
15 minutes each

○ Move

○ Clear

○ Connect

○ Love

5:00 ....
6:00 ....
7:00 ....
8:00 ....
9:00 ....
10:00 ....
11:00 ....
12:00 ....
1:00 ....
2:00 ....
3:00 ....
4:00 ....
5:00 ....
6:00 ....
7:00 ....
8:00 ....
9:00 ....
10:00 ....
11:00 ....

Visualization of Mission Goals

Mission Goal #1: ....

Mission Goal #2: ....

Mission Goal #3: ....

Evening Energy Questions

What went great today? (Wins and Celebrations)

....

....

....

....

What would I do differently tomorrow?

....

....

....

....

Ⓢ Ⓜ Ⓣ Ⓦ Ⓣ Ⓕ Ⓢ   Date _____ / _____

Morning Energy Questions

Energy

Daily Power Word:

_____

Physical Goal

Today, I will care and nurture
my body by:

_____

_____

_____

Mindset

Today, I'm grateful for:

_____

_____

Heartset

What can I do for others today?

_____

_____

Daily Core Four

15 minutes each

○ Move

○ Clear

○ Connect

○ Love

5:00 _____
6:00 _____
7:00 _____
8:00 _____
9:00 _____
10:00 _____
11:00 _____
12:00 _____
1:00 _____
2:00 _____
3:00 _____
4:00 _____
5:00 _____
6:00 _____
7:00 _____
8:00 _____
9:00 _____
10:00 _____
11:00 _____

Visualization of Mission Goals

Mission Goal #1: _____

Mission Goal #2: _____

Mission Goal #3: _____

Evening Energy Questions

What went great today? (Wins and Celebrations)

_____
_____
_____
_____

What would I do differently tomorrow?

_____
_____
_____
_____

Ⓢ Ⓜ Ⓣ Ⓦ Ⓣ Ⓕ Ⓢ   Date _____ / _____

Morning Energy Questions

Energy

Daily Power Word:

_____

Physical Goal

Today, I will care and nurture
my body by:

_____

_____

_____

Mindset

Today, I'm grateful for:

_____

_____

_____

Heartset

What can I do for others today?

_____

_____

_____

Daily Core Four

15 minutes each

○ Move

○ Clear

○ Connect

○ Love

5:00 _____
6:00 _____
7:00 _____
8:00 _____
9:00 _____
10:00 _____
11:00 _____
12:00 _____
1:00 _____
2:00 _____
3:00 _____
4:00 _____
5:00 _____
6:00 _____
7:00 _____
8:00 _____
9:00 _____
10:00 _____
11:00 _____

Visualization of Mission Goals

Mission Goal #1: _____

Mission Goal #2: _____

Mission Goal #3: _____

Evening Energy Questions

What went great today? (Wins and Celebrations)
_____
_____
_____
_____

What would I do differently tomorrow?
_____
_____
_____
_____

Ⓢ Ⓜ Ⓣ Ⓦ Ⓣ Ⓕ Ⓢ   Date _____ / _____

Morning Energy Questions

Energy

Daily Power Word:

_____

Physical Goal

Today, I will care and nurture
my body by:

_____

_____

_____

Mindset

Today, I'm grateful for:

_____

_____

_____

Heartset

What can I do for others today?

_____

_____

_____

Daily Core Four
15 minutes each

○ Move

○ Clear

○ Connect

○ Love

5:00 _____
6:00 _____
7:00 _____
8:00 _____
9:00 _____
10:00 _____
11:00 _____
12:00 _____
1:00 _____
2:00 _____
3:00 _____
4:00 _____
5:00 _____
6:00 _____
7:00 _____
8:00 _____
9:00 _____
10:00 _____
11:00 _____

Visualization of Mission Goals

Mission Goal #1: _____

Mission Goal #2: _____

Mission Goal #3: _____

Evening Energy Questions

What went great today? (Wins and Celebrations)

_____
_____
_____
_____

What would I do differently tomorrow?

_____
_____
_____
_____

Ⓢ Ⓜ Ⓣ Ⓦ Ⓣ Ⓕ Ⓢ   Date _____ / _____

Morning Energy Questions

Energy

Daily Power Word:

Physical Goal

Today, I will care and nurture
my body by:

Mindset

Today, I'm grateful for:

Heartset

What can I do for others today?

Daily Core Four

15 minutes each

○ Move
○ Clear
○ Connect
○ Love

5:00
6:00
7:00
8:00
9:00
10:00
11:00
12:00
1:00
2:00
3:00
4:00
5:00
6:00
7:00
8:00
9:00
10:00
11:00

Visualization of Mission Goals

Mission Goal #1:

Mission Goal #2:

Mission Goal #3:

Evening Energy Questions

What went great today? (Wins and Celebrations)

What would I do differently tomorrow?

Ⓢ Ⓜ Ⓣ Ⓦ Ⓣ Ⓕ Ⓢ   Date _____ / _____

Morning Energy Questions

Energy

Daily Power Word:

_____

Physical Goal

Today, I will care and nurture
my body by:

_____

_____

_____

Mindset

Today, I'm grateful for:

_____

_____

_____

Heartset

What can I do for others today?

_____

_____

_____

Daily Core Four

15 minutes each

○ Move

○ Clear

○ Connect

○ Love

5:00 _____
6:00 _____
7:00 _____
8:00 _____
9:00 _____
10:00 _____
11:00 _____
12:00 _____
1:00 _____
2:00 _____
3:00 _____
4:00 _____
5:00 _____
6:00 _____
7:00 _____
8:00 _____
9:00 _____
10:00 _____
11:00 _____

Visualization of Mission Goals

Mission Goal #1: ....

Mission Goal #2: ....

Mission Goal #3: ....

Evening Energy Questions

What went great today? (Wins and Celebrations)
....
....
....
....

What would I do differently tomorrow?
....
....
....
....

WEEK FOUR

LIfe shrinks or expands in proportion to one's courage.
–Anais Nin

#LitOnLife

Weekly Vision

WEEK

Week of: _____ / _____

Weekly Power Word:

How can I step into this intention this week?

Must Do List: Events and Deadlines

Must Do This Week	Schedule Time or Due Date	Estimate Time to Complete

Brain Dump:

Write down everything currently on your mind that is not due this week.

Item	Mission Goal or Devil's Vortex?	Due Date/Desired Completion Date	Estimated Time to Complete	Automate/Delegate Eliminate/Schedule

Connections You Would Like to Grow This Week:

....
....
....

Weekly Visualizations

Goal   How would it feel?

1: ....

2: ....

3: ....

Weekly Review

WEEK

Week of: _____ / _____

Weekly Reflections:

Wins, Celebrations, Highlights

....
....
....

Lowlights, Lessons Learned

....
....
....

What thoughts, actions and habits worked well this week?

....
....
....

What thoughts, actions and habits do you want to change?

....
....
....

Weekly Power Question

What would the person you want to be do now?

....
....
....
....

Ⓢ Ⓜ Ⓣ Ⓦ Ⓣ Ⓕ Ⓢ   Date _____ / _____

Morning Energy Questions

Energy

Daily Power Word:

Physical Goal

Today, I will care and nurture
my body by:

Mindset

Today, I'm grateful for:

Heartset

What can I do for others today?

Daily Core Four

15 minutes each

○ Move
○ Clear
○ Connect
○ Love

5:00
6:00
7:00
8:00
9:00
10:00
11:00
12:00
1:00
2:00
3:00
4:00
5:00
6:00
7:00
8:00
9:00
10:00
11:00

Visualization of Mission Goals

Mission Goal #1: ....

Mission Goal #2: ....

Mission Goal #3: ....

Evening Energy Questions

What went great today? (Wins and Celebrations)
....
....
....
....

What would I do differently tomorrow?
....
....
....
....

Ⓢ Ⓜ Ⓣ Ⓦ Ⓣ Ⓕ Ⓢ   Date _____ / _____

Morning Energy Questions

Energy

Daily Power Word:

_____

Physical Goal

Today, I will care and nurture
my body by:

_____

_____

_____

Mindset

Today, I'm grateful for:

_____

_____

_____

Heartset

What can I do for others today?

_____

_____

_____

Daily Core Four

15 minutes each

○ Move
○ Clear
○ Connect
○ Love

5:00 _____
6:00 _____
7:00 _____
8:00 _____
9:00 _____
10:00 _____
11:00 _____
12:00 _____
1:00 _____
2:00 _____
3:00 _____
4:00 _____
5:00 _____
6:00 _____
7:00 _____
8:00 _____
9:00 _____
10:00 _____
11:00 _____

Visualization of Mission Goals

Mission Goal #1: _____

Mission Goal #2: _____

Mission Goal #3: _____

Evening Energy Questions

What went great today? (Wins and Celebrations)

_____

_____

_____

_____

_____

What would I do differently tomorrow?

_____

_____

_____

_____

Ⓢ Ⓜ Ⓣ Ⓦ Ⓣ Ⓕ Ⓢ   Date _____ / _____

Morning Energy Questions
Energy
Daily Power Word:
_____

Physical Goal
Today, I will care and nurture
my body by:
_____
_____
_____

Mindset
Today, I'm grateful for:
_____
_____
_____

Heartset
What can I do for others today?
_____
_____
_____

Daily Core Four
15 minutes each
- ○ Move
- ○ Clear
- ○ Connect
- ○ Love

5:00 _____
6:00 _____
7:00 _____
8:00 _____
9:00 _____
10:00 _____
11:00 _____
12:00 _____
1:00 _____
2:00 _____
3:00 _____
4:00 _____
5:00 _____
6:00 _____
7:00 _____
8:00 _____
9:00 _____
10:00 _____
11:00 _____

Visualization of Mission Goals

Mission Goal #1: _____

Mission Goal #2: _____

Mission Goal #3: _____

Evening Energy Questions

What went great today? (Wins and Celebrations)

_____
_____
_____
_____

What would I do differently tomorrow?

_____
_____
_____
_____

Ⓢ Ⓜ Ⓣ Ⓦ Ⓣ Ⓕ Ⓢ   Date _____/_____

Morning Energy Questions

Energy

Daily Power Word:

_____

Physical Goal

Today, I will care and nurture
my body by:

_____

_____

_____

Mindset

Today, I'm grateful for:

_____

_____

_____

Heartset

What can I do for others today?

_____

_____

_____

Daily Core Four

15 minutes each

- ○ Move
- ○ Clear
- ○ Connect
- ○ Love

5:00 _____
6:00 _____
7:00 _____
8:00 _____
9:00 _____
10:00 _____
11:00 _____
12:00 _____
1:00 _____
2:00 _____
3:00 _____
4:00 _____
5:00 _____
6:00 _____
7:00 _____
8:00 _____
9:00 _____
10:00 _____
11:00 _____

Visualization of Mission Goals

Mission Goal #1: ....

Mission Goal #2: ....

Mission Goal #3: ....

Evening Energy Questions

What went great today? (Wins and Celebrations)

....

....

....

....

What would I do differently tomorrow?

....

....

....

....

Ⓢ Ⓜ Ⓣ Ⓦ Ⓣ Ⓕ Ⓢ   Date _____ / _____

Morning Energy Questions

Energy

Daily Power Word:

_____

Physical Goal

Today, I will care and nurture
my body by:

_____

_____

_____

Mindset

Today, I'm grateful for:

_____

_____

_____

Heartset

What can I do for others today?

_____

_____

_____

Daily Core Four

15 minutes each

○ Move

○ Clear

○ Connect

○ Love

5:00 _____
6:00 _____
7:00 _____
8:00 _____
9:00 _____
10:00 _____
11:00 _____
12:00 _____
1:00 _____
2:00 _____
3:00 _____
4:00 _____
5:00 _____
6:00 _____
7:00 _____
8:00 _____
9:00 _____
10:00 _____
11:00 _____

Visualization of Mission Goals

Mission Goal #1: ....

Mission Goal #2: ....

Mission Goal #3: ....

Evening Energy Questions

What went great today? (Wins and Celebrations)

....
....
....
....
....

What would I do differently tomorrow?

....
....
....
....
....

Ⓢ Ⓜ Ⓣ Ⓦ Ⓣ Ⓕ Ⓢ   Date _____ / _____

Morning Energy Questions

Energy

Daily Power Word:

_____

Physical Goal

Today, I will care and nurture
my body by:

_____

_____

Mindset

Today, I'm grateful for:

_____

_____

_____

Heartset

What can I do for others today?

_____

_____

_____

Daily Core Four
15 minutes each

○ Move
○ Clear
○ Connect
○ Love

5:00 _____
6:00 _____
7:00 _____
8:00 _____
9:00 _____
10:00 _____
11:00 _____
12:00 _____
1:00 _____
2:00 _____
3:00 _____
4:00 _____
5:00 _____
6:00 _____
7:00 _____
8:00 _____
9:00 _____
10:00 _____
11:00 _____

Visualization of Mission Goals

Mission Goal #1: ....

Mission Goal #2: ....

Mission Goal #3: ....

Evening Energy Questions

What went great today? (Wins and Celebrations)

....
....
....
....

What would I do differently tomorrow?

....
....
....
....

Ⓢ Ⓜ Ⓣ Ⓦ Ⓣ Ⓕ Ⓢ   Date _____ / _____

Morning Energy Questions

Energy

Daily Power Word:

....

Physical Goal

Today, I will care and nurture
my body by:

....

....

....

Mindset

Today, I'm grateful for:

....

....

....

Heartset

What can I do for others today?

....

....

....

Daily Core Four

15 minutes each

○ Move

○ Clear

○ Connect

○ Love

5:00 ....
6:00 ....
7:00 ....
8:00 ....
9:00 ....
10:00 ....
11:00 ....
12:00 ....
1:00 ....
2:00 ....
3:00 ....
4:00 ....
5:00 ....
6:00 ....
7:00 ....
8:00 ....
9:00 ....
10:00 ....
11:00 ....

Visualization of Mission Goals

Mission Goal #1: ....

Mission Goal #2: ....

Mission Goal #3: ....

Evening Energy Questions

What went great today? (Wins and Celebrations)
....
....
....
....

What would I do differently tomorrow?
....
....
....
....

WEEK FIVE

Connect
to the part
of yourself
that is always
Rising.

#LitOnLIfe

Weekly Vision

WEEK

Week of: _____ / _____

Weekly Power Word:

....

How can I step into this intention this week?

....

....

....

Must Do List: Events and Deadlines

Must Do This Week	Schedule Time or Due Date	Estimate Time to Complete

Brain Dump:

Write down everything currently on your mind that is not due this week.

Item	Mission Goal or Devil's Vortex?	Due Date/Desired Completion Date	Estimated Time to Complete	Automate/Delegate Eliminate/Schedule

Connections You Would Like to Grow This Week:

....

....

....

Weekly Visualizations

Goal   How would it feel?

1: ....

2: ....

3: ....

Weekly Review

WEEK

Week of: _____ / _____

Weekly Reflections:

Wins, Celebrations, Highlights

....

....

Lowlights, Lessons Learned

....

....

What thoughts, actions and habits worked well this week?

....

....

What thoughts, actions and habits do you want to change?

....

....

Weekly Power Question

I feel most energized when…?

....

....

....

Ⓢ Ⓜ Ⓣ Ⓦ Ⓣ Ⓕ Ⓢ   Date _____ / _____

Morning Energy Questions

Energy

Daily Power Word:

_____

Physical Goal

Today, I will care and nurture
my body by:

_____

_____

_____

Mindset

Today, I'm grateful for:

_____

_____

_____

Heartset

What can I do for others today?

_____

_____

Daily Core Four

15 minutes each

○ Move
○ Clear
○ Connect
○ Love

5:00 _____
6:00 _____
7:00 _____
8:00 _____
9:00 _____
10:00 _____
11:00 _____
12:00 _____
1:00 _____
2:00 _____
3:00 _____
4:00 _____
5:00 _____
6:00 _____
7:00 _____
8:00 _____
9:00 _____
10:00 _____
11:00 _____

Visualization of Mission Goals

Mission Goal #1: ....

Mission Goal #2: ....

Mission Goal #3: ....

Evening Energy Questions

What went great today? (Wins and Celebrations)
....
....
....
....
....

What would I do differently tomorrow?
....
....
....
....
....

(S) (M) (T) (W) (T) (F) (S)   Date _____ / _____

Morning Energy Questions

Energy

Daily Power Word:

_____

Physical Goal

Today, I will care and nurture
my body by:

_____

_____

_____

Mindset

Today, I'm grateful for:

_____

_____

_____

Heartset

What can I do for others today?

_____

_____

_____

Daily Core Four

15 minutes each

○ Move
○ Clear
○ Connect
○ Love

5:00 _____
6:00 _____
7:00 _____
8:00 _____
9:00 _____
10:00 _____
11:00 _____
12:00 _____
1:00 _____
2:00 _____
3:00 _____
4:00 _____
5:00 _____
6:00 _____
7:00 _____
8:00 _____
9:00 _____
10:00 _____
11:00 _____

Visualization of Mission Goals

Mission Goal #1: _____

Mission Goal #2: _____

Mission Goal #3: _____

Evening Energy Questions

What went great today? (Wins and Celebrations)

_____
_____
_____
_____

What would I do differently tomorrow?

_____
_____
_____
_____

Ⓢ Ⓜ Ⓣ Ⓦ Ⓣ Ⓕ Ⓢ   Date _____ / _____

Morning Energy Questions

Energy

Daily Power Word:

....

Physical Goal

Today, I will care and nurture
my body by:

....

....

....

Mindset

Today, I'm grateful for:

....

....

....

Heartset

What can I do for others today?

....

....

....

Daily Core Four

15 minutes each

○ Move
○ Clear
○ Connect
○ Love

5:00 ....
6:00 ....
7:00 ....
8:00 ....
9:00 ....
10:00 ....
11:00 ....
12:00 ....
1:00 ....
2:00 ....
3:00 ....
4:00 ....
5:00 ....
6:00 ....
7:00 ....
8:00 ....
9:00 ....
10:00 ....
11:00 ....

Visualization of Mission Goals

Mission Goal #1: ....

Mission Goal #2: ....

Mission Goal #3: ....

Evening Energy Questions

What went great today? (Wins and Celebrations)

....
....
....
....
....

What would I do differently tomorrow?

....
....
....
....
....

Ⓢ Ⓜ Ⓣ Ⓦ Ⓣ Ⓕ Ⓢ   Date _____ / _____

Morning Energy Questions

Energy

Daily Power Word:

....

Physical Goal

Today, I will care and nurture
my body by:

....

....

....

Mindset

Today, I'm grateful for:

....

....

....

Heartset

What can I do for others today?

....

....

....

Daily Core Four

15 minutes each

○ Move

○ Clear

○ Connect

○ Love

5:00 ....
6:00 ....
7:00 ....
8:00 ....
9:00 ....
10:00 ....
11:00 ....
12:00 ....
1:00 ....
2:00 ....
3:00 ....
4:00 ....
5:00 ....
6:00 ....
7:00 ....
8:00 ....
9:00 ....
10:00 ....
11:00 ....

Visualization of Mission Goals

Mission Goal #1: ....

Mission Goal #2: ....

Mission Goal #3: ....

Evening Energy Questions

What went great today? (Wins and Celebrations)

....

....

....

....

What would I do differently tomorrow?

....

....

....

....

Ⓢ Ⓜ Ⓣ Ⓦ Ⓣ Ⓕ Ⓢ   Date _____ / _____

Morning Energy Questions

Energy

Daily Power Word:

....

Physical Goal

Today, I will care and nurture
my body by:

....

....

....

Mindset

Today, I'm grateful for:

....

....

....

Heartset

What can I do for others today?

....

....

....

Daily Core Four

15 minutes each

○ Move

○ Clear

○ Connect

○ Love

5:00 ....
6:00 ....
7:00 ....
8:00 ....
9:00 ....
10:00 ....
11:00 ....
12:00 ....
1:00 ....
2:00 ....
3:00 ....
4:00 ....
5:00 ....
6:00 ....
7:00 ....
8:00 ....
9:00 ....
10:00 ....
11:00 ....

Visualization of Mission Goals

Mission Goal #1: ....

Mission Goal #2: ....

Mission Goal #3: ....

Evening Energy Questions

What went great today? (Wins and Celebrations)
....
....
....
....

What would I do differently tomorrow?
....
....
....
....

Ⓢ Ⓜ Ⓣ Ⓦ Ⓣ Ⓕ Ⓢ   Date _____ / _____

Morning Energy Questions

Energy

Daily Power Word:

_____

Physical Goal

Today, I will care and nurture
my body by:

_____

_____

_____

Mindset

Today, I'm grateful for:

_____

_____

_____

Heartset

What can I do for others today?

_____

_____

_____

Daily Core Four

15 minutes each

○ Move
○ Clear
○ Connect
○ Love

5:00 _____
6:00 _____
7:00 _____
8:00 _____
9:00 _____
10:00 _____
11:00 _____
12:00 _____
1:00 _____
2:00 _____
3:00 _____
4:00 _____
5:00 _____
6:00 _____
7:00 _____
8:00 _____
9:00 _____
10:00 _____
11:00 _____

Visualization of Mission Goals

Mission Goal #1: ....

Mission Goal #2: ....

Mission Goal #3: ....

Evening Energy Questions

What went great today? (Wins and Celebrations)

....
....
....
....

What would I do differently tomorrow?

....
....
....
....

Ⓢ Ⓜ Ⓣ Ⓦ Ⓣ Ⓕ Ⓢ   Date _____ / _____

Morning Energy Questions

Energy

Daily Power Word:

_____

Physical Goal

Today, I will care and nurture
my body by:

_____

_____

_____

Mindset

Today, I'm grateful for:

_____

_____

_____

Heartset

What can I do for others today?

_____

_____

_____

Daily Core Four

15 minutes each

○ Move

○ Clear

○ Connect

○ Love

5:00	
6:00	
7:00	
8:00	
9:00	
10:00	
11:00	
12:00	
1:00	
2:00	
3:00	
4:00	
5:00	
6:00	
7:00	
8:00	
9:00	
10:00	
11:00	

Visualization of Mission Goals

Mission Goal #1: ....

Mission Goal #2: ....

Mission Goal #3: ....

Evening Energy Questions

What went great today? (Wins and Celebrations)

....

....

....

....

What would I do differently tomorrow?

....

....

....

....

WEEK SIX

Abundance
is something
we tune into.

.#LitOnLIfe

Weekly Vision

WEEK

Week of: _____ / _____

Weekly Power Word:

How can I step into this intention this week?

Must Do List: Events and Deadlines

Must Do This Week	Schedule Time or Due Date	Estimate Time to Complete

Brain Dump:
Write down everything currently on your mind that is not due this week.

Item	Mission Goal or Devil's Vortex?	Due Date/Desired Completion Date	Estimated Time to Complete	Automate/Delegate Eliminate/Schedule

Connections You Would Like to Grow This Week:

....

....

....

Weekly Visualizations

Goal   How would it feel?

1: ....

2: ....

3: ....

Weekly Review

WEEK

Week of: _____ / _____

Weekly Reflections:

Wins, Celebrations, Highlights

....
....
....

Lowlights, Lessons Learned

....
....
....

What thoughts, actions and habits worked well this week?

....
....
....

What thoughts, actions and habits do you want to change?

....
....
....

Weekly Power Question

Are you using your time wisely? If not, how can you change?

....
....
....
....

Ⓢ Ⓜ Ⓣ Ⓦ Ⓣ Ⓕ Ⓢ   Date _____ / _____

Morning Energy Questions

Energy

Daily Power Word:

_____

Physical Goal

Today, I will care and nurture
my body by:

_____

_____

_____

Mindset

Today, I'm grateful for:

_____

_____

_____

Heartset

What can I do for others today?

_____

_____

Daily Core Four

15 minutes each

○ Move

○ Clear

○ Connect

○ Love

5:00 _____

6:00 _____

7:00 _____

8:00 _____

9:00 _____

10:00 _____

11:00 _____

12:00 _____

1:00 _____

2:00 _____

3:00 _____

4:00 _____

5:00 _____

6:00 _____

7:00 _____

8:00 _____

9:00 _____

10:00 _____

11:00 _____

Visualization of Mission Goals

Mission Goal #1: ....

Mission Goal #2: ....

Mission Goal #3: ....

Evening Energy Questions

What went great today? (Wins and Celebrations)

....
....
....
....

What would I do differently tomorrow?

....
....
....
....

Ⓢ Ⓜ Ⓣ Ⓦ Ⓣ Ⓕ Ⓢ   Date _____ / _____

Morning Energy Questions

Energy

Daily Power Word:

....

Physical Goal

Today, I will care and nurture
my body by:

....

....

....

Mindset

Today, I'm grateful for:

....

....

....

Heartset

What can I do for others today?

....

....

....

Daily Core Four

15 minutes each

○ Move

○ Clear

○ Connect

○ Love

5:00 ....
6:00 ....
7:00 ....
8:00 ....
9:00 ....
10:00 ....
11:00 ....
12:00 ....
1:00 ....
2:00 ....
3:00 ....
4:00 ....
5:00 ....
6:00 ....
7:00 ....
8:00 ....
9:00 ....
10:00 ....
11:00 ....

Visualization of Mission Goals

Mission Goal #1: _____

Mission Goal #2: _____

Mission Goal #3: _____

Evening Energy Questions

What went great today? (Wins and Celebrations)
_____
_____
_____
_____

What would I do differently tomorrow?
_____
_____
_____
_____

Ⓢ Ⓜ Ⓣ Ⓦ Ⓣ Ⓕ Ⓢ   Date _____ / _____

Morning Energy Questions

Energy

Daily Power Word:

_____

Physical Goal

Today, I will care and nurture
my body by:

_____

_____

Mindset

Today, I'm grateful for:

_____

_____

Heartset

What can I do for others today?

_____

_____

Daily Core Four

15 minutes each

○ Move
○ Clear
○ Connect
○ Love

5:00 _____
6:00 _____
7:00 _____
8:00 _____
9:00 _____
10:00 _____
11:00 _____
12:00 _____
1:00 _____
2:00 _____
3:00 _____
4:00 _____
5:00 _____
6:00 _____
7:00 _____
8:00 _____
9:00 _____
10:00 _____
11:00 _____

Visualization of Mission Goals

Mission Goal #1: ....

Mission Goal #2: ....

Mission Goal #3: ....

Evening Energy Questions

What went great today? (Wins and Celebrations)

....
....
....
....
....

What would I do differently tomorrow?

....
....
....
....
....

Ⓢ Ⓜ Ⓣ Ⓦ Ⓣ Ⓕ Ⓢ   Date _____ / _____

Morning Energy Questions
Energy
Daily Power Word:

Physical Goal
Today, I will care and nurture
my body by:

Mindset
Today, I'm grateful for:

Heartset
What can I do for others today?

Daily Core Four
15 minutes each
- ○ Move
- ○ Clear
- ○ Connect
- ○ Love

5:00 _____
6:00 _____
7:00 _____
8:00 _____
9:00 _____
10:00 _____
11:00 _____
12:00 _____
1:00 _____
2:00 _____
3:00 _____
4:00 _____
5:00 _____
6:00 _____
7:00 _____
8:00 _____
9:00 _____
10:00 _____
11:00 _____

Visualization of Mission Goals

Mission Goal #1: ....

Mission Goal #2: ....

Mission Goal #3: ....

Evening Energy Questions

What went great today? (Wins and Celebrations)

....

....

....

....

....

What would I do differently tomorrow?

....

....

....

....

....

Ⓢ Ⓜ Ⓣ Ⓦ Ⓣ Ⓕ Ⓢ   Date _____/_____

Morning Energy Questions

Energy

Daily Power Word:

....

Physical Goal

Today, I will care and nurture
my body by:

....

....

....

Mindset

Today, I'm grateful for:

....

....

....

Heartset

What can I do for others today?

....

....

....

Daily Core Four

15 minutes each

○ Move

○ Clear

○ Connect

○ Love

5:00 ....

6:00 ....

7:00 ....

8:00 ....

9:00 ....

10:00 ....

11:00 ....

12:00 ....

1:00 ....

2:00 ....

3:00 ....

4:00 ....

5:00 ....

6:00 ....

7:00 ....

8:00 ....

9:00 ....

10:00 ....

11:00 ....

Visualization of Mission Goals

Mission Goal #1: ....

Mission Goal #2: ....

Mission Goal #3: ....

Evening Energy Questions

What went great today? (Wins and Celebrations)

....

....

....

....

....

What would I do differently tomorrow?

....

....

....

....

....

Ⓢ Ⓜ Ⓣ Ⓦ Ⓣ Ⓕ Ⓢ   Date _____ / _____

Morning Energy Questions

Energy

Daily Power Word:

_____

Physical Goal

Today, I will care and nurture
my body by:

_____

_____

_____

Mindset

Today, I'm grateful for:

_____

_____

_____

Heartset

What can I do for others today?

_____

_____

_____

Daily Core Four

15 minutes each

○ Move
○ Clear
○ Connect
○ Love

5:00 _____
6:00 _____
7:00 _____
8:00 _____
9:00 _____
10:00 _____
11:00 _____
12:00 _____
1:00 _____
2:00 _____
3:00 _____
4:00 _____
5:00 _____
6:00 _____
7:00 _____
8:00 _____
9:00 _____
10:00 _____
11:00 _____

Visualization of Mission Goals

Mission Goal #1: ....

Mission Goal #2: ....

Mission Goal #3: ....

Evening Energy Questions

What went great today? (Wins and Celebrations)

....
....
....
....

What would I do differently tomorrow?

....
....
....
....

S M T W T F S

Date _____ /_____

Morning Energy Questions

Energy

Daily Power Word:

....

Physical Goal

Today, I will care and nurture
my body by:

....

....

....

Mindset

Today, I'm grateful for:

....

....

....

Heartset

What can I do for others today?

....

....

....

Daily Core Four

15 minutes each

○ Move
○ Clear
○ Connect
○ Love

5:00 ....
6:00 ....
7:00 ....
8:00 ....
9:00 ....
10:00 ....
11:00 ....
12:00 ....
1:00 ....
2:00 ....
3:00 ....
4:00 ....
5:00 ....
6:00 ....
7:00 ....
8:00 ....
9:00 ....
10:00 ....
11:00 ....

Visualization of Mission Goals

Mission Goal #1: ....

Mission Goal #2: ....

Mission Goal #3: ....

Evening Energy Questions

What went great today? (Wins and Celebrations)

....

....

....

....

....

What would I do differently tomorrow?

....

....

....

....

....

WEEK SEVEN

Create
Miracles
with
Your Life!

.#LitOnLIfe

Weekly Vision

WEEK

Week of: _____ / _____

Weekly Power Word:

....

How can I step into this intention this week?

....

....

Must Do List: Events and Deadlines

Must Do This Week	Schedule Time or Due Date	Estimate Time to Complete

Brain Dump:

Write down everything currently on your mind that is not due this week.

Item	Mission Goal or Devil's Vortex?	Due Date/Desired Completion Date	Estimated Time to Complete	Automate/Delegate Eliminate/Schedule

Connections You Would Like to Grow This Week:

....

....

....

Weekly Visualizations

Goal   How would it feel?

1: ....

2: ....

3: ....

Weekly Review

WEEK

Week of: _____ / _____

Weekly Reflections:

Wins, Celebrations, Highlights

....

....

....

Lowlights, Lessons Learned

....

....

....

What thoughts, actions and habits worked well this week?

....

....

....

What thoughts, actions and habits do you want to change?

....

....

....

Weekly Power Question

Make a list of 10 things that make you smile.

....

....

....

....

Ⓢ Ⓜ Ⓣ Ⓦ Ⓣ Ⓕ Ⓢ   Date _____ / _____

Morning Energy Questions

Energy

Daily Power Word:

_____

Physical Goal

Today, I will care and nurture
my body by:

_____

_____

_____

Mindset

Today, I'm grateful for:

_____

_____

_____

Heartset

What can I do for others today?

_____

_____

Daily Core Four

15 minutes each

○ Move

○ Clear

○ Connect

○ Love

5:00 _____
6:00 _____
7:00 _____
8:00 _____
9:00 _____
10:00 _____
11:00 _____
12:00 _____
1:00 _____
2:00 _____
3:00 _____
4:00 _____
5:00 _____
6:00 _____
7:00 _____
8:00 _____
9:00 _____
10:00 _____
11:00 _____

Visualization of Mission Goals

Mission Goal #1: ....

Mission Goal #2: ....

Mission Goal #3: ....

Evening Energy Questions

What went great today? (Wins and Celebrations)

....

....

....

....

What would I do differently tomorrow?

....

....

....

....

Ⓢ Ⓜ Ⓣ Ⓦ Ⓣ Ⓕ Ⓢ   Date _____ / _____

Morning Energy Questions

Energy

Daily Power Word:

_____

Physical Goal

Today, I will care and nurture
my body by:

_____

_____

Mindset

Today, I'm grateful for:

_____

_____

Heartset

What can I do for others today?

_____

_____

Daily Core Four
15 minutes each
- ○ Move
- ○ Clear
- ○ Connect
- ○ Love

5:00 _____
6:00 _____
7:00 _____
8:00 _____
9:00 _____
10:00 _____
11:00 _____
12:00 _____
1:00 _____
2:00 _____
3:00 _____
4:00 _____
5:00 _____
6:00 _____
7:00 _____
8:00 _____
9:00 _____
10:00 _____
11:00 _____

Visualization of Mission Goals

Mission Goal #1: ....

Mission Goal #2: ....

Mission Goal #3: ....

Evening Energy Questions

What went great today? (Wins and Celebrations)

....

....

....

....

What would I do differently tomorrow?

....

....

....

....

Ⓢ Ⓜ Ⓣ Ⓦ Ⓣ Ⓕ Ⓢ   Date _____ / _____

Morning Energy Questions

Energy

Daily Power Word:

_____

Physical Goal

Today, I will care and nurture
my body by:

_____

_____

_____

Mindset

Today, I'm grateful for:

_____

_____

_____

Heartset

What can I do for others today?

_____

_____

_____

Daily Core Four
15 minutes each

○ Move
○ Clear
○ Connect
○ Love

5:00 _____
6:00 _____
7:00 _____
8:00 _____
9:00 _____
10:00 _____
11:00 _____
12:00 _____
1:00 _____
2:00 _____
3:00 _____
4:00 _____
5:00 _____
6:00 _____
7:00 _____
8:00 _____
9:00 _____
10:00 _____
11:00 _____

Visualization of Mission Goals

Mission Goal #1: ....

Mission Goal #2: ....

Mission Goal #3: ....

Evening Energy Questions

What went great today? (Wins and Celebrations)
....
....
....
....

What would I do differently tomorrow?
....
....
....
....

Ⓢ Ⓜ Ⓣ Ⓦ Ⓣ Ⓕ Ⓢ   Date _____ / _____

Morning Energy Questions

Energy

Daily Power Word:

Physical Goal

Today, I will care and nurture
my body by:

Mindset

Today, I'm grateful for:

Heartset

What can I do for others today?

Daily Core Four

15 minutes each

○ Move

○ Clear

○ Connect

○ Love

5:00 _____
6:00 _____
7:00 _____
8:00 _____
9:00 _____
10:00 _____
11:00 _____
12:00 _____
1:00 _____
2:00 _____
3:00 _____
4:00 _____
5:00 _____
6:00 _____
7:00 _____
8:00 _____
9:00 _____
10:00 _____
11:00 _____

Visualization of Mission Goals

Mission Goal #1:

Mission Goal #2:

Mission Goal #3:

Evening Energy Questions

What went great today? (Wins and Celebrations)

What would I do differently tomorrow?

Ⓢ Ⓜ Ⓣ Ⓦ Ⓣ Ⓕ Ⓢ   Date _____ / _____

Morning Energy Questions

Energy

Daily Power Word:

_____

Physical Goal

Today, I will care and nurture
my body by:

_____

_____

Mindset

Today, I'm grateful for:

_____

_____

_____

Heartset

What can I do for others today?

_____

_____

Daily Core Four

15 minutes each

○ Move
○ Clear
○ Connect
○ Love

5:00 _____
6:00 _____
7:00 _____
8:00 _____
9:00 _____
10:00 _____
11:00 _____
12:00 _____
1:00 _____
2:00 _____
3:00 _____
4:00 _____
5:00 _____
6:00 _____
7:00 _____
8:00 _____
9:00 _____
10:00 _____
11:00 _____

Visualization of Mission Goals

Mission Goal #1: ....

Mission Goal #2: ....

Mission Goal #3: ....

Evening Energy Questions

What went great today? (Wins and Celebrations)

....

....

....

....

What would I do differently tomorrow?

....

....

....

....

Ⓢ Ⓜ Ⓣ Ⓦ Ⓣ Ⓕ Ⓢ   Date _____ / _____

Morning Energy Questions

Energy

Daily Power Word:

....

Physical Goal

Today, I will care and nurture
my body by:

....

....

....

Mindset

Today, I'm grateful for:

....

....

....

Heartset

What can I do for others today?

....

....

....

Daily Core Four

15 minutes each

○ Move

○ Clear

○ Connect

○ Love

5:00 ....
6:00 ....
7:00 ....
8:00 ....
9:00 ....
10:00 ....
11:00 ....
12:00 ....
1:00 ....
2:00 ....
3:00 ....
4:00 ....
5:00 ....
6:00 ....
7:00 ....
8:00 ....
9:00 ....
10:00 ....
11:00 ....

Visualization of Mission Goals

Mission Goal #1: ....

Mission Goal #2: ....

Mission Goal #3: ....

Evening Energy Questions

What went great today? (Wins and Celebrations)

....

....

....

....

What would I do differently tomorrow?

....

....

....

....

Ⓢ Ⓜ Ⓣ Ⓦ Ⓣ Ⓕ Ⓢ Date _____/_____

Morning Energy Questions

Energy
Daily Power Word:

_____

Physical Goal
Today, I will care and nurture
my body by:

_____

_____

_____

Mindset
Today, I'm grateful for:

_____

_____

_____

Heartset
What can I do for others today?

_____

_____

_____

Daily Core Four
15 minutes each
- ○ Move
- ○ Clear
- ○ Connect
- ○ Love

5:00 _____
6:00 _____
7:00 _____
8:00 _____
9:00 _____
10:00 _____
11:00 _____
12:00 _____
1:00 _____
2:00 _____
3:00 _____
4:00 _____
5:00 _____
6:00 _____
7:00 _____
8:00 _____
9:00 _____
10:00 _____
11:00 _____

Visualization of Mission Goals

Mission Goal #1: ....

Mission Goal #2: ....

Mission Goal #3: ....

Evening Energy Questions

What went great today? (Wins and Celebrations)

....

....

....

....

What would I do differently tomorrow?

....

....

....

....

WEEK EIGHT

Happiness is an inside job.

.#LitOnLIfe

Weekly Vision

WEEK

Week of: _____ / _____

Weekly Power Word:

....

How can I step into this intention this week?

....

....

....

Must Do List: Events and Deadlines

Must Do This Week	Schedule Time or Due Date	Estimate Time to Complete

Brain Dump:

Write down everything currently on your mind that is not due this week.

Item	Mission Goal or Devil's Vortex?	Due Date/Desired Completion Date	Estimated Time to Complete	Automate/Delegate Eliminate/Schedule

Connections You Would Like to Grow This Week:

....

....

....

Weekly Visualizations

Goal   How would it feel?

1: ....

2: ....

3: ....

Weekly Review

WEEK 8

Week of: _____/_____

Weekly Reflections:

Wins, Celebrations, Highlights

....
....
....

Lowlights, Lessons Learned

....
....
....

What thoughts, actions and habits worked well this week?

....
....
....

What thoughts, actions and habits do you want to change?

....
....
....

Weekly Power Question

The words you like to live by are....?

....
....
....
....

Ⓢ Ⓜ Ⓣ Ⓦ Ⓣ Ⓕ Ⓢ   Date _____ / _____

Morning Energy Questions

Energy

Daily Power Word:

_____

Physical Goal

Today, I will care and nurture
my body by:

_____

_____

Mindset

Today, I'm grateful for:

_____

_____

Heartset

What can I do for others today?

_____

_____

Daily Core Four

15 minutes each

○ Move
○ Clear
○ Connect
○ Love

5:00 _____
6:00 _____
7:00 _____
8:00 _____
9:00 _____
10:00 _____
11:00 _____
12:00 _____
1:00 _____
2:00 _____
3:00 _____
4:00 _____
5:00 _____
6:00 _____
7:00 _____
8:00 _____
9:00 _____
10:00 _____
11:00 _____

Visualization of Mission Goals

Mission Goal #1:

Mission Goal #2:

Mission Goal #3:

Evening Energy Questions

What went great today? (Wins and Celebrations)

What would I do differently tomorrow?

Ⓢ Ⓜ Ⓣ Ⓦ Ⓣ Ⓕ Ⓢ Date _____ / _____

Morning Energy Questions

Energy

Daily Power Word:

_____

Physical Goal

Today, I will care and nurture
my body by:

_____

_____

_____

Mindset

Today, I'm grateful for:

_____

_____

_____

Heartset

What can I do for others today?

_____

_____

Daily Core Four

15 minutes each

○ Move
○ Clear
○ Connect
○ Love

5:00 _____
6:00 _____
7:00 _____
8:00 _____
9:00 _____
10:00 _____
11:00 _____
12:00 _____
1:00 _____
2:00 _____
3:00 _____
4:00 _____
5:00 _____
6:00 _____
7:00 _____
8:00 _____
9:00 _____
10:00 _____
11:00 _____

Visualization of Mission Goals

Mission Goal #1: _____

Mission Goal #2: _____

Mission Goal #3: _____

Evening Energy Questions

What went great today? (Wins and Celebrations)

_____

_____

_____

_____

What would I do differently tomorrow?

_____

_____

_____

Ⓢ Ⓜ Ⓣ Ⓦ Ⓣ Ⓕ Ⓢ   Date _____ / _____

Morning Energy Questions

Energy

Daily Power Word:

....

Physical Goal

Today, I will care and nurture
my body by:

....

....

....

Mindset

Today, I'm grateful for:

....

....

....

Heartset

What can I do for others today?

....

....

....

Daily Core Four

15 minutes each

○ Move

○ Clear

○ Connect

○ Love

5:00 ....
6:00 ....
7:00 ....
8:00 ....
9:00 ....
10:00 ....
11:00 ....
12:00 ....
1:00 ....
2:00 ....
3:00 ....
4:00 ....
5:00 ....
6:00 ....
7:00 ....
8:00 ....
9:00 ....
10:00 ....
11:00 ....

Visualization of Mission Goals

Mission Goal #1:

Mission Goal #2:

Mission Goal #3:

Evening Energy Questions

What went great today? (Wins and Celebrations)

What would I do differently tomorrow?

(S) (M) (T) (W) (T) (F) (S)   Date _____ / _____

Morning Energy Questions

Energy

Daily Power Word:

....

Physical Goal

Today, I will care and nurture
my body by:

....

....

....

Mindset

Today, I'm grateful for:

....

....

....

Heartset

What can I do for others today?

....

....

....

Daily Core Four

15 minutes each

○ Move

○ Clear

○ Connect

○ Love

5:00 ....
6:00 ....
7:00 ....
8:00 ....
9:00 ....
10:00 ....
11:00 ....
12:00 ....
1:00 ....
2:00 ....
3:00 ....
4:00 ....
5:00 ....
6:00 ....
7:00 ....
8:00 ....
9:00 ....
10:00 ....
11:00 ....

Visualization of Mission Goals

Mission Goal #1: ....

Mission Goal #2: ....

Mission Goal #3: ....

Evening Energy Questions

What went great today? (Wins and Celebrations)
....
....
....
....

What would I do differently tomorrow?
....
....
....
....

(S) (M) (T) (W) (T) (F) (S)   Date _____ / _____

Morning Energy Questions

Energy

Daily Power Word:

_____

Physical Goal

Today, I will care and nurture
my body by:

_____

_____

_____

Mindset

Today, I'm grateful for:

_____

_____

_____

Heartset

What can I do for others today?

_____

_____

_____

Daily Core Four
15 minutes each

○ Move
○ Clear
○ Connect
○ Love

5:00 _____
6:00 _____
7:00 _____
8:00 _____
9:00 _____
10:00 _____
11:00 _____
12:00 _____
1:00 _____
2:00 _____
3:00 _____
4:00 _____
5:00 _____
6:00 _____
7:00 _____
8:00 _____
9:00 _____
10:00 _____
11:00 _____

Visualization of Mission Goals

Mission Goal #1:

Mission Goal #2:

Mission Goal #3:

Evening Energy Questions

What went great today? (Wins and Celebrations)

What would I do differently tomorrow?

Ⓢ Ⓜ Ⓣ Ⓦ Ⓣ Ⓕ Ⓢ   Date _____ / _____

Morning Energy Questions

Energy

Daily Power Word:

....

Physical Goal

Today, I will care and nurture
my body by:

....

....

Mindset

Today, I'm grateful for:

....

....

....

Heartset

What can I do for others today?

....

....

....

Daily Core Four

15 minutes each

○ Move
○ Clear
○ Connect
○ Love

5:00 ....
6:00 ....
7:00 ....
8:00 ....
9:00 ....
10:00 ....
11:00 ....
12:00 ....
1:00 ....
2:00 ....
3:00 ....
4:00 ....
5:00 ....
6:00 ....
7:00 ....
8:00 ....
9:00 ....
10:00 ....
11:00 ....

Visualization of Mission Goals

Mission Goal #1: ....

Mission Goal #2: ....

Mission Goal #3: ....

Evening Energy Questions

What went great today? (Wins and Celebrations)
....
....
....
....

What would I do differently tomorrow?
....
....
....
....

Ⓢ Ⓜ Ⓣ Ⓦ Ⓣ Ⓕ Ⓢ   Date _____ / _____

Morning Energy Questions

Energy

Daily Power Word:

_____

Physical Goal

Today, I will care and nurture
my body by:

_____

_____

Mindset

Today, I'm grateful for:

_____

_____

Heartset

What can I do for others today?

_____

_____

Daily Core Four
15 minutes each

○ Move
○ Clear
○ Connect
○ Love

5:00 _____
6:00 _____
7:00 _____
8:00 _____
9:00 _____
10:00 _____
11:00 _____
12:00 _____
1:00 _____
2:00 _____
3:00 _____
4:00 _____
5:00 _____
6:00 _____
7:00 _____
8:00 _____
9:00 _____
10:00 _____
11:00 _____

Visualization of Mission Goals

Mission Goal #1: ....

Mission Goal #2: ....

Mission Goal #3: ....

Evening Energy Questions

What went great today? (Wins and Celebrations)
....
....
....
....

What would I do differently tomorrow?
....
....
....
....

WEEK NINE

You are
always one
choice away
from a totally
different life.

#LitOnLIfe

Weekly Vision

WEEK

Week of: _____ / _____

Weekly Power Word:

....

How can I step into this intention this week?

....

....

Must Do List: Events and Deadlines

Must Do This Week	Schedule Time or Due Date	Estimate Time to Complete

Brain Dump:

Write down everything currently on your mind that is not due this week.

Item	Mission Goal or Devil's Vortex?	Due Date/Desired Completion Date	Estimated Time to Complete	Automate/Delegate Eliminate/Schedule

Connections You Would Like to Grow This Week:

....

....

....

Weekly Visualizations

Goal   How would it feel?

1: ....

2: ....

3: ....

Weekly Review

Week of: _____ / _____

Weekly Reflections:

Wins, Celebrations, Highlights

....
....
....

Lowlights, Lessons Learned

....
....
....

What thoughts, actions and habits worked well this week?

....
....
....

What thoughts, actions and habits do you want to change?

....
....
....

Weekly Power Question

How do you have to think and act now to be satisfied on your deathbed?

....
....
....
....

Ⓢ Ⓜ Ⓣ Ⓦ Ⓣ Ⓕ Ⓢ   Date _____ / _____

Morning Energy Questions

Energy

Daily Power Word:

_____

Physical Goal

Today, I will care and nurture
my body by:

_____

_____

_____

Mindset

Today, I'm grateful for:

_____

_____

_____

Heartset

What can I do for others today?

_____

_____

_____

Daily Core Four

15 minutes each

○ Move

○ Clear

○ Connect

○ Love

5:00 _____
6:00 _____
7:00 _____
8:00 _____
9:00 _____
10:00 _____
11:00 _____
12:00 _____
1:00 _____
2:00 _____
3:00 _____
4:00 _____
5:00 _____
6:00 _____
7:00 _____
8:00 _____
9:00 _____
10:00 _____
11:00 _____

Visualization of Mission Goals

Mission Goal #1: ....

Mission Goal #2: ....

Mission Goal #3: ....

Evening Energy Questions

What went great today? (Wins and Celebrations)
....
....
....
....

What would I do differently tomorrow?
....
....
....
....

Ⓢ Ⓜ Ⓣ Ⓦ Ⓣ Ⓕ Ⓢ   Date _____ / _____

Morning Energy Questions

Energy

Daily Power Word:

_____

Physical Goal

Today, I will care and nurture
my body by:

_____

_____

Mindset

Today, I'm grateful for:

_____

_____

Heartset

What can I do for others today?

_____

_____

Daily Core Four

15 minutes each

○ Move

○ Clear

○ Connect

○ Love

5:00 _____
6:00 _____
7:00 _____
8:00 _____
9:00 _____
10:00 _____
11:00 _____
12:00 _____
1:00 _____
2:00 _____
3:00 _____
4:00 _____
5:00 _____
6:00 _____
7:00 _____
8:00 _____
9:00 _____
10:00 _____
11:00 _____

Visualization of Mission Goals

Mission Goal #1: ....

Mission Goal #2: ....

Mission Goal #3: ....

Evening Energy Questions

What went great today? (Wins and Celebrations)

....

....

....

....

What would I do differently tomorrow?

....

....

....

....

Ⓢ Ⓜ Ⓣ Ⓦ Ⓣ Ⓕ Ⓢ   Date _____ / _____

Morning Energy Questions

Energy

Daily Power Word:

Physical Goal

Today, I will care and nurture
my body by:

Mindset

Today, I'm grateful for:

Heartset

What can I do for others today?

Daily Core Four

15 minutes each

○ Move
○ Clear
○ Connect
○ Love

5:00
6:00
7:00
8:00
9:00
10:00
11:00
12:00
1:00
2:00
3:00
4:00
5:00
6:00
7:00
8:00
9:00
10:00
11:00

Visualization of Mission Goals

Mission Goal #1: ....

Mission Goal #2: ....

Mission Goal #3: ....

Evening Energy Questions

What went great today? (Wins and Celebrations)
....
....
....
....

What would I do differently tomorrow?
....
....
....
....

Ⓢ Ⓜ Ⓣ Ⓦ Ⓣ Ⓕ Ⓢ   Date _____ / _____

Morning Energy Questions

Energy

Daily Power Word:

_____

Physical Goal

Today, I will care and nurture
my body by:

_____

_____

Mindset

Today, I'm grateful for:

_____

_____

_____

Heartset

What can I do for others today?

_____

_____

_____

Daily Core Four

15 minutes each

○ Move
○ Clear
○ Connect
○ Love

5:00 _____
6:00 _____
7:00 _____
8:00 _____
9:00 _____
10:00 _____
11:00 _____
12:00 _____
1:00 _____
2:00 _____
3:00 _____
4:00 _____
5:00 _____
6:00 _____
7:00 _____
8:00 _____
9:00 _____
10:00 _____
11:00 _____

Visualization of Mission Goals

Mission Goal #1: ....

Mission Goal #2: ....

Mission Goal #3: ....

Evening Energy Questions

What went great today? (Wins and Celebrations)

....
....
....
....

What would I do differently tomorrow?

....
....
....
....

(S) (M) (T) (W) (T) (F) (S) Date _____ / _____

Morning Energy Questions

Energy

Daily Power Word:

_____

Physical Goal

Today, I will care and nurture
my body by:

_____

_____

_____

Mindset

Today, I'm grateful for:

_____

_____

_____

Heartset

What can I do for others today?

_____

_____

_____

Daily Core Four

15 minutes each

- ○ Move
- ○ Clear
- ○ Connect
- ○ Love

5:00 _____
6:00 _____
7:00 _____
8:00 _____
9:00 _____
10:00 _____
11:00 _____
12:00 _____
1:00 _____
2:00 _____
3:00 _____
4:00 _____
5:00 _____
6:00 _____
7:00 _____
8:00 _____
9:00 _____
10:00 _____
11:00 _____

Visualization of Mission Goals

Mission Goal #1: ....

Mission Goal #2: ....

Mission Goal #3: ....

Evening Energy Questions

What went great today? (Wins and Celebrations)
....
....
....
....

What would I do differently tomorrow?
....
....
....
....

Ⓢ Ⓜ Ⓣ Ⓦ Ⓣ Ⓕ Ⓢ   Date _____ / _____

Morning Energy Questions

Energy

Daily Power Word:

_____

Physical Goal

Today, I will care and nurture
my body by:

_____

_____

_____

Mindset

Today, I'm grateful for:

_____

_____

_____

Heartset

What can I do for others today?

_____

_____

_____

Daily Core Four

15 minutes each

○ Move
○ Clear
○ Connect
○ Love

5:00 _____
6:00 _____
7:00 _____
8:00 _____
9:00 _____
10:00 _____
11:00 _____
12:00 _____
1:00 _____
2:00 _____
3:00 _____
4:00 _____
5:00 _____
6:00 _____
7:00 _____
8:00 _____
9:00 _____
10:00 _____
11:00 _____

Visualization of Mission Goals

Mission Goal #1: _____

Mission Goal #2: _____

Mission Goal #3: _____

Evening Energy Questions

What went great today? (Wins and Celebrations)

_____

_____

_____

_____

What would I do differently tomorrow?

_____

_____

_____

_____

Ⓢ Ⓜ Ⓣ Ⓦ Ⓣ Ⓕ Ⓢ   Date _____/_____

Morning Energy Questions

Energy

Daily Power Word:

....

Physical Goal

Today, I will care and nurture
my body by:

....

....

....

Mindset

Today, I'm grateful for:

....

....

....

Heartset

What can I do for others today?

....

....

....

Daily Core Four
15 minutes each

○ Move
○ Clear
○ Connect
○ Love

5:00 ....
6:00 ....
7:00 ....
8:00 ....
9:00 ....
10:00 ....
11:00 ....
12:00 ....
1:00 ....
2:00 ....
3:00 ....
4:00 ....
5:00 ....
6:00 ....
7:00 ....
8:00 ....
9:00 ....
10:00 ....
11:00 ....

Visualization of Mission Goals

Mission Goal #1:

Mission Goal #2:

Mission Goal #3:

Evening Energy Questions

What went great today? (Wins and Celebrations)

What would I do differently tomorrow?

WEEK TEN

Success is loving life and daring to live it.

#LitOnLIfe

Weekly Vision

WEEK

Week of: _____/_____

Weekly Power Word:

....

How can I step into this intention this week?

....

....

Must Do List: Events and Deadlines

Must Do This Week	Schedule Time or Due Date	Estimate Time to Complete

Brain Dump:

Write down everything currently on your mind that is not due this week.

Item	Mission Goal or Devil's Vortex?	Due Date/Desired Completion Date	Estimated Time to Complete	Automate/Delegate Eliminate/Schedule

Connections You Would Like to Grow This Week:

....

....

....

Weekly Visualizations

Goal   How would it feel?

1: ....

2: ....

3: ....

Weekly Review

Week of: _____ / _____

Weekly Reflections:

Wins, Celebrations, Highlights

....
....
....

Lowlights, Lessons Learned

....
....
....

What thoughts, actions and habits worked well this week?

....
....
....

What thoughts, actions and habits do you want to change?

....
....
....

Weekly Power Question

When did you last push the boundaries of your comfort zone?

....
....
....
....

Ⓢ Ⓜ Ⓣ Ⓦ Ⓣ Ⓕ Ⓢ   Date _____ / _____

Morning Energy Questions

Energy

Daily Power Word:

_____

Physical Goal

Today, I will care and nurture
my body by:

_____

_____

_____

Mindset

Today, I'm grateful for:

_____

_____

_____

Heartset

What can I do for others today?

_____

_____

_____

Daily Core Four

15 minutes each

○ Move

○ Clear

○ Connect

○ Love

5:00 _____
6:00 _____
7:00 _____
8:00 _____
9:00 _____
10:00 _____
11:00 _____
12:00 _____
1:00 _____
2:00 _____
3:00 _____
4:00 _____
5:00 _____
6:00 _____
7:00 _____
8:00 _____
9:00 _____
10:00 _____
11:00 _____

Visualization of Mission Goals

Mission Goal #1: _____

Mission Goal #2: _____

Mission Goal #3: _____

Evening Energy Questions

What went great today? (Wins and Celebrations)
_____
_____
_____
_____

What would I do differently tomorrow?
_____
_____
_____
_____

Ⓢ Ⓜ Ⓣ Ⓦ Ⓣ Ⓕ Ⓢ   Date _____ / _____

Morning Energy Questions

Energy

Daily Power Word:

_____

Physical Goal

Today, I will care and nurture
my body by:

_____

_____

_____

Mindset

Today, I'm grateful for:

_____

_____

_____

Heartset

What can I do for others today?

_____

_____

_____

Daily Core Four

15 minutes each

○ Move
○ Clear
○ Connect
○ Love

5:00 _____
6:00 _____
7:00 _____
8:00 _____
9:00 _____
10:00 _____
11:00 _____
12:00 _____
1:00 _____
2:00 _____
3:00 _____
4:00 _____
5:00 _____
6:00 _____
7:00 _____
8:00 _____
9:00 _____
10:00 _____
11:00 _____

Visualization of Mission Goals

Mission Goal #1:

Mission Goal #2:

Mission Goal #3:

Evening Energy Questions

What went great today? (Wins and Celebrations)

What would I do differently tomorrow?

Ⓢ Ⓜ Ⓣ Ⓦ Ⓣ Ⓕ Ⓢ   Date _____/_____

Morning Energy Questions

Energy

Daily Power Word:

_____

Physical Goal

Today, I will care and nurture
my body by:

_____

_____

Mindset

Today, I'm grateful for:

_____

_____

_____

Heartset

What can I do for others today?

_____

_____

_____

Daily Core Four

15 minutes each

○ Move

○ Clear

○ Connect

○ Love

5:00 _____

6:00 _____

7:00 _____

8:00 _____

9:00 _____

10:00 _____

11:00 _____

12:00 _____

1:00 _____

2:00 _____

3:00 _____

4:00 _____

5:00 _____

6:00 _____

7:00 _____

8:00 _____

9:00 _____

10:00 _____

11:00 _____

Visualization of Mission Goals

Mission Goal #1:

Mission Goal #2:

Mission Goal #3:

Evening Energy Questions

What went great today? (Wins and Celebrations)

What would I do differently tomorrow?

Ⓢ Ⓜ Ⓣ Ⓦ Ⓣ Ⓕ Ⓢ   Date _____/_____

Morning Energy Questions

Energy

Daily Power Word:

_____

Physical Goal

Today, I will care and nurture
my body by:

_____

_____

_____

Mindset

Today, I'm grateful for:

_____

_____

_____

Heartset

What can I do for others today?

_____

_____

_____

Daily Core Four

15 minutes each

○ Move

○ Clear

○ Connect

○ Love

5:00 _____
6:00 _____
7:00 _____
8:00 _____
9:00 _____
10:00 _____
11:00 _____
12:00 _____
1:00 _____
2:00 _____
3:00 _____
4:00 _____
5:00 _____
6:00 _____
7:00 _____
8:00 _____
9:00 _____
10:00 _____
11:00 _____

Visualization of Mission Goals

Mission Goal #1: ....

Mission Goal #2: ....

Mission Goal #3: ....

Evening Energy Questions

What went great today? (Wins and Celebrations)

....
....
....
....

What would I do differently tomorrow?

....
....
....
....

Ⓢ Ⓜ Ⓣ Ⓦ Ⓣ Ⓕ Ⓢ   Date _____ / _____

Morning Energy Questions

Energy

Daily Power Word:

_____

Physical Goal

Today, I will care and nurture
my body by:

_____

_____

_____

Mindset

Today, I'm grateful for:

_____

_____

_____

Heartset

What can I do for others today?

_____

_____

_____

Daily Core Four

15 minutes each

○ Move
○ Clear
○ Connect
○ Love

5:00 _____
6:00 _____
7:00 _____
8:00 _____
9:00 _____
10:00 _____
11:00 _____
12:00 _____
1:00 _____
2:00 _____
3:00 _____
4:00 _____
5:00 _____
6:00 _____
7:00 _____
8:00 _____
9:00 _____
10:00 _____
11:00 _____

Visualization of Mission Goals

Mission Goal #1: ....

Mission Goal #2: ....

Mission Goal #3: ....

Evening Energy Questions

What went great today? (Wins and Celebrations)

....

....

....

....

....

What would I do differently tomorrow?

....

....

....

....

....

Ⓢ Ⓜ Ⓣ Ⓦ Ⓣ Ⓕ Ⓢ   Date _____ /_____

Morning Energy Questions

Energy

Daily Power Word:

_____

Physical Goal

Today, I will care and nurture
my body by:

_____

_____

_____

Mindset

Today, I'm grateful for:

_____

_____

_____

Heartset

What can I do for others today?

_____

_____

_____

Daily Core Four

15 minutes each

○ Move

○ Clear

○ Connect

○ Love

5:00 _____
6:00 _____
7:00 _____
8:00 _____
9:00 _____
10:00 _____
11:00 _____
12:00 _____
1:00 _____
2:00 _____
3:00 _____
4:00 _____
5:00 _____
6:00 _____
7:00 _____
8:00 _____
9:00 _____
10:00 _____
11:00 _____

Visualization of Mission Goals

Mission Goal #1: ....

Mission Goal #2: ....

Mission Goal #3: ....

Evening Energy Questions

What went great today? (Wins and Celebrations)

....
....
....
....

What would I do differently tomorrow?

....
....
....
....

Ⓢ Ⓜ Ⓣ Ⓦ Ⓣ Ⓕ Ⓢ   Date _____/_____

Morning Energy Questions

Energy

Daily Power Word:

....

Physical Goal

Today, I will care and nurture
my body by:

....

....

....

Mindset

Today, I'm grateful for:

....

....

....

Heartset

What can I do for others today?

....

....

....

Daily Core Four

15 minutes each

○ Move

○ Clear

○ Connect

○ Love

5:00 ....
6:00 ....
7:00 ....
8:00 ....
9:00 ....
10:00 ....
11:00 ....
12:00 ....
1:00 ....
2:00 ....
3:00 ....
4:00 ....
5:00 ....
6:00 ....
7:00 ....
8:00 ....
9:00 ....
10:00 ....
11:00 ....

Visualization of Mission Goals

Mission Goal #1:

Mission Goal #2:

Mission Goal #3:

Evening Energy Questions

What went great today? (Wins and Celebrations)

What would I do differently tomorrow?

WEEK ELEVEN

The difference
between
you and who
you want to be
is what you do.

#LitOnLIfe

Weekly Vision

WEEK 11

Week of: _____ / _____

Weekly Power Word:

How can I step into this intention this week?

Must Do List: Events and Deadlines

Must Do This Week	Schedule Time or Due Date	Estimate Time to Complete

Brain Dump:

Write down everything currently on your mind that is not due this week.

Item	Mission Goal or Devil's Vortex?	Due Date/Desired Completion Date	Estimated Time to Complete	Automate/Delegate Eliminate/Schedule

Connections You Would Like to Grow This Week:

....

....

....

Weekly Visualizations

Goal   How would it feel?

1: ....

2: ....

3: ....

Weekly Review

WEEK 11

Week of: _____ / _____

Weekly Reflections:

Wins, Celebrations, Highlights

....
....
....

Lowlights, Lessons Learned

....
....
....

What thoughts, actions and habits worked well this week?

....
....
....

What thoughts, actions and habits do you want to change?

....
....
....

Weekly Power Question

What is life asking of you?

....
....
....
....

Ⓢ Ⓜ Ⓣ Ⓦ Ⓣ Ⓕ Ⓢ   Date _____ / _____

Morning Energy Questions

Energy

Daily Power Word:

_____

Physical Goal

Today, I will care and nurture
my body by:

_____

_____

Mindset

Today, I'm grateful for:

_____

_____

Heartset

What can I do for others today?

_____

_____

Daily Core Four

15 minutes each

○ Move
○ Clear
○ Connect
○ Love

5:00 _____
6:00 _____
7:00 _____
8:00 _____
9:00 _____
10:00 _____
11:00 _____
12:00 _____
1:00 _____
2:00 _____
3:00 _____
4:00 _____
5:00 _____
6:00 _____
7:00 _____
8:00 _____
9:00 _____
10:00 _____
11:00 _____

Visualization of Mission Goals

Mission Goal #1: ....

Mission Goal #2: ....

Mission Goal #3: ....

Evening Energy Questions

What went great today? (Wins and Celebrations)

....

....

....

....

What would I do differently tomorrow?

....

....

....

....

Ⓢ Ⓜ Ⓣ Ⓦ Ⓣ Ⓕ Ⓢ   Date _____ / _____

Morning Energy Questions

Energy

Daily Power Word:

_____

Physical Goal

Today, I will care and nurture
my body by:

_____

_____

_____

Mindset

Today, I'm grateful for:

_____

_____

_____

Heartset

What can I do for others today?

_____

_____

_____

Daily Core Four

15 minutes each

○ Move
○ Clear
○ Connect
○ Love

5:00 _____
6:00 _____
7:00 _____
8:00 _____
9:00 _____
10:00 _____
11:00 _____
12:00 _____
1:00 _____
2:00 _____
3:00 _____
4:00 _____
5:00 _____
6:00 _____
7:00 _____
8:00 _____
9:00 _____
10:00 _____
11:00 _____

Visualization of Mission Goals

Mission Goal #1: _____

Mission Goal #2: _____

Mission Goal #3: _____

Evening Energy Questions

What went great today? (Wins and Celebrations)

_____
_____
_____
_____

What would I do differently tomorrow?

_____
_____
_____
_____

Ⓢ Ⓜ Ⓣ Ⓦ Ⓣ Ⓕ Ⓢ   Date _____ / _____

Morning Energy Questions

Energy

Daily Power Word:

....

Physical Goal

Today, I will care and nurture
my body by:

....

....

....

Mindset

Today, I'm grateful for:

....

....

....

Heartset

What can I do for others today?

....

....

....

Daily Core Four

15 minutes each

○ Move

○ Clear

○ Connect

○ Love

5:00 ....

6:00 ....

7:00 ....

8:00 ....

9:00 ....

10:00 ....

11:00 ....

12:00 ....

1:00 ....

2:00 ....

3:00 ....

4:00 ....

5:00 ....

6:00 ....

7:00 ....

8:00 ....

9:00 ....

10:00 ....

11:00 ....

Visualization of Mission Goals

Mission Goal #1: ....

Mission Goal #2: ....

Mission Goal #3: ....

Evening Energy Questions

What went great today? (Wins and Celebrations)

....

....

....

....

What would I do differently tomorrow?

....

....

....

....

S M T W T F S   Date _____ / _____

Morning Energy Questions

Energy
Daily Power Word:
....

Physical Goal
Today, I will care and nurture
my body by:
....
....
....

Mindset
Today, I'm grateful for:
....
....
....

Heartset
What can I do for others today?
....
....
....

Daily Core Four
15 minutes each
○ Move
○ Clear
○ Connect
○ Love

5:00 ....
6:00 ....
7:00 ....
8:00 ....
9:00 ....
10:00 ....
11:00 ....
12:00 ....
1:00 ....
2:00 ....
3:00 ....
4:00 ....
5:00 ....
6:00 ....
7:00 ....
8:00 ....
9:00 ....
10:00 ....
11:00 ....

Visualization of Mission Goals

Mission Goal #1: ....

Mission Goal #2: ....

Mission Goal #3: ....

Evening Energy Questions

What went great today? (Wins and Celebrations)

....

....

....

....

What would I do differently tomorrow?

....

....

....

....

Ⓢ Ⓜ Ⓣ Ⓦ Ⓣ Ⓕ Ⓢ   Date _____ / _____

Morning Energy Questions

Energy

Daily Power Word:

_____

Physical Goal

Today, I will care and nurture
my body by:

_____

_____

Mindset

Today, I'm grateful for:

_____

_____

Heartset

What can I do for others today?

_____

_____

Daily Core Four

15 minutes each

○ Move
○ Clear
○ Connect
○ Love

5:00 _____
6:00 _____
7:00 _____
8:00 _____
9:00 _____
10:00 _____
11:00 _____
12:00 _____
1:00 _____
2:00 _____
3:00 _____
4:00 _____
5:00 _____
6:00 _____
7:00 _____
8:00 _____
9:00 _____
10:00 _____
11:00 _____

Visualization of Mission Goals

Mission Goal #1:

Mission Goal #2:

Mission Goal #3:

Evening Energy Questions

What went great today? (Wins and Celebrations)

What would I do differently tomorrow?

(S) (M) (T) (W) (T) (F) (S)   Date _____ / _____

Morning Energy Questions

Energy

Daily Power Word:

_____

Physical Goal

Today, I will care and nurture
my body by:

_____

_____

_____

Mindset

Today, I'm grateful for:

_____

_____

_____

Heartset

What can I do for others today?

_____

_____

Daily Core Four

15 minutes each

○ Move

○ Clear

○ Connect

○ Love

5:00 _____
6:00 _____
7:00 _____
8:00 _____
9:00 _____
10:00 _____
11:00 _____
12:00 _____
1:00 _____
2:00 _____
3:00 _____
4:00 _____
5:00 _____
6:00 _____
7:00 _____
8:00 _____
9:00 _____
10:00 _____
11:00 _____

Visualization of Mission Goals

Mission Goal #1:

Mission Goal #2:

Mission Goal #3:

Evening Energy Questions

What went great today? (Wins and Celebrations)

What would I do differently tomorrow?

Ⓢ Ⓜ Ⓣ Ⓦ Ⓣ Ⓕ Ⓢ   Date _____ / _____

Morning Energy Questions

Energy

Daily Power Word:

....

Physical Goal

Today, I will care and nurture
my body by:

....

....

Mindset

Today, I'm grateful for:

....

....

Heartset

What can I do for others today?

....

....

Daily Core Four

15 minutes each

○ Move

○ Clear

○ Connect

○ Love

5:00 ....

6:00 ....

7:00 ....

8:00 ....

9:00 ....

10:00 ....

11:00 ....

12:00 ....

1:00 ....

2:00 ....

3:00 ....

4:00 ....

5:00 ....

6:00 ....

7:00 ....

8:00 ....

9:00 ....

10:00 ....

11:00 ....

Visualization of Mission Goals

Mission Goal #1: ....

Mission Goal #2: ....

Mission Goal #3: ....

Evening Energy Questions

What went great today? (Wins and Celebrations)

....

....

....

....

What would I do differently tomorrow?

....

....

....

WEEK TWELVE

Keep an inner picture of abundance and your outer world will expand.

#LitOnLIfe

Weekly Vision

WEEK

Week of: _____ / _____

Weekly Power Word:

How can I step into this intention this week?

Must Do List: Events and Deadlines

Must Do This Week	Schedule Time or Due Date	Estimate Time to Complete

Brain Dump:

Write down everything currently on your mind that is not due this week.

Item	Mission Goal or Devil's Vortex?	Due Date/Desired Completion Date	Estimated Time to Complete	Automate/Delegate Eliminate/Schedule

Connections You Would Like to Grow This Week:

....

....

....

Weekly Visualizations

Goal   How would it feel?

1: ....

2: ....

3: ....

Weekly Review

WEEK

Week of: _____ / _____

Weekly Reflections:

Wins, Celebrations, Highlights

....

....

....

Lowlights, Lessons Learned

....

....

....

What thoughts, actions and habits worked well this week?

....

....

....

What thoughts, actions and habits do you want to change?

....

....

....

Weekly Power Question

"What matters most to you in life?"

....

....

....

....

Ⓢ Ⓜ Ⓣ Ⓦ Ⓣ Ⓕ Ⓢ   Date _____ / _____

Morning Energy Questions

Energy

Daily Power Word:

Physical Goal

Today, I will care and nurture
my body by:

Mindset

Today, I'm grateful for:

Heartset

What can I do for others today?

Daily Core Four
15 minutes each

○ Move
○ Clear
○ Connect
○ Love

5:00
6:00
7:00
8:00
9:00
10:00
11:00
12:00
1:00
2:00
3:00
4:00
5:00
6:00
7:00
8:00
9:00
10:00
11:00

Visualization of Mission Goals

Mission Goal #1:

Mission Goal #2:

Mission Goal #3:

Evening Energy Questions

What went great today? (Wins and Celebrations)

What would I do differently tomorrow?

Ⓢ Ⓜ Ⓣ Ⓦ Ⓣ Ⓕ Ⓢ   Date _____ / _____

Morning Energy Questions

Energy

Daily Power Word:

_____

Physical Goal

Today, I will care and nurture
my body by:

_____

_____

_____

Mindset

Today, I'm grateful for:

_____

_____

_____

Heartset

What can I do for others today?

_____

_____

_____

Daily Core Four

15 minutes each

- ○ Move
- ○ Clear
- ○ Connect
- ○ Love

5:00 _____
6:00 _____
7:00 _____
8:00 _____
9:00 _____
10:00 _____
11:00 _____
12:00 _____
1:00 _____
2:00 _____
3:00 _____
4:00 _____
5:00 _____
6:00 _____
7:00 _____
8:00 _____
9:00 _____
10:00 _____
11:00 _____

Visualization of Mission Goals

Mission Goal #1:

Mission Goal #2:

Mission Goal #3:

Evening Energy Questions

What went great today? (Wins and Celebrations)

What would I do differently tomorrow?

Ⓢ Ⓜ Ⓣ Ⓦ Ⓣ Ⓕ Ⓢ   Date _____ / _____

Morning Energy Questions

Energy

Daily Power Word:

....

Physical Goal

Today, I will care and nurture
my body by:

....

....

....

Mindset

Today, I'm grateful for:

....

....

....

Heartset

What can I do for others today?

....

....

Daily Core Four

15 minutes each

○ Move
○ Clear
○ Connect
○ Love

5:00	
6:00	
7:00	
8:00	
9:00	
10:00	
11:00	
12:00	
1:00	
2:00	
3:00	
4:00	
5:00	
6:00	
7:00	
8:00	
9:00	
10:00	
11:00	

Visualization of Mission Goals

Mission Goal #1: ....

Mission Goal #2: ....

Mission Goal #3: ....

Evening Energy Questions

What went great today? (Wins and Celebrations)
....
....
....
....
....

What would I do differently tomorrow?
....
....
....
....
....

Ⓢ Ⓜ Ⓣ Ⓦ Ⓣ Ⓕ Ⓢ   Date _____/_____

Morning Energy Questions

Energy

Daily Power Word:

_____

Physical Goal

Today, I will care and nurture
my body by:

_____

_____

_____

Mindset

Today, I'm grateful for:

_____

_____

_____

Heartset

What can I do for others today?

_____

_____

Daily Core Four

15 minutes each

○ Move
○ Clear
○ Connect
○ Love

5:00 _____
6:00 _____
7:00 _____
8:00 _____
9:00 _____
10:00 _____
11:00 _____
12:00 _____
1:00 _____
2:00 _____
3:00 _____
4:00 _____
5:00 _____
6:00 _____
7:00 _____
8:00 _____
9:00 _____
10:00 _____
11:00 _____

Visualization of Mission Goals

Mission Goal #1: _____

Mission Goal #2: _____

Mission Goal #3: _____

Evening Energy Questions

What went great today? (Wins and Celebrations)

_____

_____

_____

_____

What would I do differently tomorrow?

_____

_____

_____

_____

Ⓢ Ⓜ Ⓣ Ⓦ Ⓣ Ⓕ Ⓢ   Date _____ / _____

Morning Energy Questions

Energy

Daily Power Word:

....

Physical Goal

Today, I will care and nurture
my body by:

....

....

....

Mindset

Today, I'm grateful for:

....

....

....

Heartset

What can I do for others today?

....

....

....

Daily Core Four

15 minutes each

○ Move

○ Clear

○ Connect

○ Love

5:00	
6:00	
7:00	
8:00	
9:00	
10:00	
11:00	
12:00	
1:00	
2:00	
3:00	
4:00	
5:00	
6:00	
7:00	
8:00	
9:00	
10:00	
11:00	

Visualization of Mission Goals

Mission Goal #1: ....

Mission Goal #2: ....

Mission Goal #3: ....

Evening Energy Questions

What went great today? (Wins and Celebrations)

....

....

....

....

What would I do differently tomorrow?

....

....

....

....

(S) (M) (T) (W) (T) (F) (S)   Date _____ / _____

Morning Energy Questions

Energy
Daily Power Word:
_____

Physical Goal
Today, I will care and nurture
my body by:
_____
_____
_____

Mindset
Today, I'm grateful for:
_____
_____
_____

Heartset
What can I do for others today?
_____
_____
_____

Daily Core Four
15 minutes each
- ○ Move
- ○ Clear
- ○ Connect
- ○ Love

5:00 _____
6:00 _____
7:00 _____
8:00 _____
9:00 _____
10:00 _____
11:00 _____
12:00 _____
1:00 _____
2:00 _____
3:00 _____
4:00 _____
5:00 _____
6:00 _____
7:00 _____
8:00 _____
9:00 _____
10:00 _____
11:00 _____

Visualization of Mission Goals

Mission Goal #1:

Mission Goal #2:

Mission Goal #3:

Evening Energy Questions

What went great today? (Wins and Celebrations)

What would I do differently tomorrow?

Ⓢ Ⓜ Ⓣ Ⓦ Ⓣ Ⓕ Ⓢ   Date _____/_____

Morning Energy Questions

Energy

Daily Power Word:

_____

Physical Goal

Today, I will care and nurture my body by:

_____

_____

Mindset

Today, I'm grateful for:

_____

_____

Heartset

What can I do for others today?

_____

_____

Daily Core Four

15 minutes each

○ Move
○ Clear
○ Connect
○ Love

5:00 _____
6:00 _____
7:00 _____
8:00 _____
9:00 _____
10:00 _____
11:00 _____
12:00 _____
1:00 _____
2:00 _____
3:00 _____
4:00 _____
5:00 _____
6:00 _____
7:00 _____
8:00 _____
9:00 _____
10:00 _____
11:00 _____

Visualization of Mission Goals

Mission Goal #1:

Mission Goal #2:

Mission Goal #3:

Evening Energy Questions

What went great today? (Wins and Celebrations)

What would I do differently tomorrow?

WEEK THIRTEEN

Imagination
is your
gateway
to success.

#LitOnLIfe

Weekly Vision

WEEK 13

Week of: _____ / _____

Weekly Power Word:

How can I step into this intention this week?

Must Do List: Events and Deadlines

Must Do This Week	Schedule Time or Due Date	Estimate Time to Complete

Brain Dump:

Write down everything currently on your mind that is not due this week.

Item	Mission Goal or Devil's Vortex?	Due Date/Desired Completion Date	Estimated Time to Complete	Automate/Delegate Eliminate/Schedule

Connections You Would Like to Grow This Week:

....
....
....

Weekly Visualizations

Goal   How would it feel?

1: ....

2: ....

3: ....

Weekly Review

WEEK

Week of: _____ / _____

Weekly Reflections:

Wins, Celebrations, Highlights

_____
_____
_____

Lowlights, Lessons Learned

_____
_____
_____

What thoughts, actions and habits worked well this week?

_____
_____
_____

What thoughts, actions and habits do you want to change?

_____
_____
_____

Weekly Power Question

How will you live, knowing that you will die?

_____
_____
_____
_____

S M T W T F S   Date _____ / _____

Morning Energy Questions

Energy

Daily Power Word:

....

Physical Goal

Today, I will care and nurture
my body by:

....

....

Mindset

Today, I'm grateful for:

....

....

Heartset

What can I do for others today?

....

....

Daily Core Four
15 minutes each

○ Move
○ Clear
○ Connect
○ Love

5:00 ....
6:00 ....
7:00 ....
8:00 ....
9:00 ....
10:00 ....
11:00 ....
12:00 ....
1:00 ....
2:00 ....
3:00 ....
4:00 ....
5:00 ....
6:00 ....
7:00 ....
8:00 ....
9:00 ....
10:00 ....
11:00 ....

Visualization of Mission Goals

Mission Goal #1:

Mission Goal #2:

Mission Goal #3:

Evening Energy Questions

What went great today? (Wins and Celebrations)

What would I do differently tomorrow?

(S) (M) (T) (W) (T) (F) (S)   Date _____ / _____

Morning Energy Questions

Energy

Daily Power Word:

_____

Physical Goal

Today, I will care and nurture
my body by:

_____

_____

_____

Mindset

Today, I'm grateful for:

_____

_____

_____

Heartset

What can I do for others today?

_____

_____

_____

Daily Core Four

15 minutes each

○ Move
○ Clear
○ Connect
○ Love

5:00 _____
6:00 _____
7:00 _____
8:00 _____
9:00 _____
10:00 _____
11:00 _____
12:00 _____
1:00 _____
2:00 _____
3:00 _____
4:00 _____
5:00 _____
6:00 _____
7:00 _____
8:00 _____
9:00 _____
10:00 _____
11:00 _____

Visualization of Mission Goals

Mission Goal #1: ....

Mission Goal #2: ....

Mission Goal #3: ....

Evening Energy Questions

What went great today? (Wins and Celebrations)

....

....

....

....

What would I do differently tomorrow?

....

....

....

....

Ⓢ Ⓜ Ⓣ Ⓦ Ⓣ Ⓕ Ⓢ   Date _____ / _____

Morning Energy Questions

Energy

Daily Power Word:

_____

Physical Goal

Today, I will care and nurture
my body by:

_____

_____

_____

Mindset

Today, I'm grateful for:

_____

_____

_____

Heartset

What can I do for others today?

_____

_____

_____

Daily Core Four

15 minutes each

○ Move
○ Clear
○ Connect
○ Love

5:00 _____
6:00 _____
7:00 _____
8:00 _____
9:00 _____
10:00 _____
11:00 _____
12:00 _____
1:00 _____
2:00 _____
3:00 _____
4:00 _____
5:00 _____
6:00 _____
7:00 _____
8:00 _____
9:00 _____
10:00 _____
11:00 _____

Visualization of Mission Goals

Mission Goal #1: ....

Mission Goal #2: ....

Mission Goal #3: ....

Evening Energy Questions

What went great today? (Wins and Celebrations)

....

....

....

....

What would I do differently tomorrow?

....

....

....

....

Ⓢ Ⓜ Ⓣ Ⓦ Ⓣ Ⓕ Ⓢ   Date _____/_____

Morning Energy Questions

Energy

Daily Power Word:

_____

Physical Goal

Today, I will care and nurture
my body by:

_____

_____

Mindset

Today, I'm grateful for:

_____

_____

Heartset

What can I do for others today?

_____

_____

Daily Core Four

15 minutes each

○ Move

○ Clear

○ Connect

○ Love

5:00 _____
6:00 _____
7:00 _____
8:00 _____
9:00 _____
10:00 _____
11:00 _____
12:00 _____
1:00 _____
2:00 _____
3:00 _____
4:00 _____
5:00 _____
6:00 _____
7:00 _____
8:00 _____
9:00 _____
10:00 _____
11:00 _____

Visualization of Mission Goals

Mission Goal #1: ....

Mission Goal #2: ....

Mission Goal #3: ....

Evening Energy Questions

What went great today? (Wins and Celebrations)

....
....
....
....

What would I do differently tomorrow?

....
....
....
....

Ⓢ Ⓜ Ⓣ Ⓦ Ⓣ Ⓕ Ⓢ   Date _____ / _____

Morning Energy Questions

Energy

Daily Power Word:

Physical Goal

Today, I will care and nurture
my body by:

Mindset

Today, I'm grateful for:

Heartset

What can I do for others today?

Daily Core Four
15 minutes each

○ Move
○ Clear
○ Connect
○ Love

5:00
6:00
7:00
8:00
9:00
10:00
11:00
12:00
1:00
2:00
3:00
4:00
5:00
6:00
7:00
8:00
9:00
10.00
11:00

Visualization of Mission Goals

Mission Goal #1: _____

Mission Goal #2: _____

Mission Goal #3: _____

Evening Energy Questions

What went great today? (Wins and Celebrations)

_____
_____
_____
_____

What would I do differently tomorrow?

_____
_____
_____
_____

Ⓢ Ⓜ Ⓣ Ⓦ Ⓣ Ⓕ Ⓢ   Date _____ / _____

Morning Energy Questions

Energy

Daily Power Word:

_____

Physical Goal

Today, I will care and nurture
my body by:

_____

_____

_____

Mindset

Today, I'm grateful for:

_____

_____

_____

Heartset

What can I do for others today?

_____

_____

_____

Daily Core Four

15 minutes each

○ Move
○ Clear
○ Connect
○ Love

5:00 _____
6:00 _____
7:00 _____
8:00 _____
9:00 _____
10:00 _____
11:00 _____
12:00 _____
1:00 _____
2:00 _____
3:00 _____
4:00 _____
5:00 _____
6:00 _____
7:00 _____
8:00 _____
9:00 _____
10:00 _____
11:00 _____

Visualization of Mission Goals

Mission Goal #1: ....

Mission Goal #2: ....

Mission Goal #3: ....

Evening Energy Questions

What went great today? (Wins and Celebrations)

....
....
....
....

What would I do differently tomorrow?

....
....
....
....

Ⓢ Ⓜ Ⓣ Ⓦ Ⓣ Ⓕ Ⓢ   Date _____ / _____

Morning Energy Questions

Energy

Daily Power Word:

_____

Physical Goal

Today, I will care and nurture
my body by:

_____

_____

_____

Mindset

Today, I'm grateful for:

_____

_____

_____

Heartset

What can I do for others today?

_____

_____

_____

Daily Core Four

15 minutes each

○ Move
○ Clear
○ Connect
○ Love

5:00 _____
6:00 _____
7:00 _____
8:00 _____
9:00 _____
10:00 _____
11:00 _____
12:00 _____
1:00 _____
2:00 _____
3:00 _____
4:00 _____
5:00 _____
6:00 _____
7:00 _____
8:00 _____
9:00 _____
10:00 _____
11:00 _____

Visualization of Mission Goals

Mission Goal #1: ....

Mission Goal #2: ....

Mission Goal #3: ....

Evening Energy Questions

What went great today? (Wins and Celebrations)

....

....

....

....

What would I do differently tomorrow?

....

....

....

....

WINS!
(HIGHLIGHTS—MOMENTS OF JOY—SUCCESSES)

Write down the wins—small and big shifts and the remarkable things you have accomplished!

- ❖ _____
- ❖ _____
- ❖ _____
- ❖ _____
- ❖ _____
- ❖ _____
- ❖ _____
- ❖ _____
- ❖ _____
- ❖ _____
- ❖ _____
- ❖ _____
- ❖ _____
- ❖ _____
- ❖ _____

www.ingramcontent.com/pod-product-compliance
Lightning Source LLC
Chambersburg PA
CBHW072145100526
44589CB00015B/2102